Hi Shan,

Thanks for demonstrating servant-hearted leadership.

Looking forward to our continued journey together.

All the best,

[illegible]

July 2016

What Others Are Saying
About Elias Kanaris and This Book

"'Authenticity' is a word thrown around too freely these days. But when you come across a leader, ambassador, and messenger who truly exemplifies the term, you are wise to sit up and listen. In *Liberating Your Leadership Potential*, Elias Kanaris not only channels the lessons of Mandela, but he reveals his own unique voice in the process. Poignant, thought-provoking, and refreshingly actionable, this is a profound guide not only to digest, but to revisit again and again."

— David Avrin, Business Speaker and
Author of *Visibility Marketing*

"Want to strengthen your leadership skills to influence others on your team to achieve more? Start here!"

— Jeff Page, Chief Executive Officer of
Kepa - The Advisers Institute

"As a senior certified consultant and speaker on international stages, I have access to some of highest quality and most ethical leaders on this planet. Elias Kanaris definitely stands out as one of those leaders because of his natural leadership talent, his ability to inspire others towards liberating mind-sets, and his ability to see the bigger picture. I highly recommend that you unlock your leadership potential with Elias Kanaris' keys to leadership."

— Landi Jac, Founder and Chairman of
The Consultant Code

"I've known Elias for some time now, and I can say he walks his talk. And even though I had already heard him share much of what he's written, I gained fresh insights as I read his book. You will too as you take this journey with him."

— Scott M. Fay, Vice President of The John Maxwell Team
and CEO of Rood Landscape Company

"When all the elements of inspired leadership converge, Elias Kanaris is the perfect storm. That was my experience in a season of tremendous growth and discovery whilst exposed to Elias' leadership. If enlarging capacity and unlocking potential is important to you, read this book. Profound influence is inevitable."

— Richie Lewis, Founding Pastor of Grace Global NZ

"Elias Kanaris has been on the journey of self-discovery and personal growth for years. In this book, he shares key principles that he has both learned and lived along the way. Grab a cup of coffee, a pad of paper, and a pen, and prepare to enjoy the journey. I know you will find many things you will want to recall for years to come."

— Paul Martinelli, President of Empowerment Mentoring

"Because Elias knows his own non-negotiables and he can apply them in his life and in his work, he's the one to show us how to find our way to effective leadership through the traits and core-values of Nelson Mandela."

— Paul ter Wal CSP, Keynote Speaker,
Author, and All-Round Good Guy

"Elias Kanaris is a committed, responsive leader with an eye for futurism and best practice. I would suggest this book is an extension of his genius and can be a stunning tool for any individual engaged in being a leader for others, in business, or in a community."

— Mike Handcock, CSP (Global), Multi-Award Winning Author, and Chairman of Rock Your Life

"Elias is not just someone with vision and passion to make a difference; he has a great and easy way of providing clarity for those wanting to make a difference in their lives. In your hands is a heart story—one that will resonate. It will provide vision, hope, clarity, and a framework for freedom and how to become all that you were created for. Get ready for new adventures as you read this impactful book."

— Tony Lynch, Founder of Keep Thinking BIG and Author of *Think BIG Leadership*

"Whenever I want to have an enlightening discussion about leadership, the colleague with whom I get in touch is Elias Kanaris. This is one of the best books I have ever read on leadership, and it is written by a gentleman who practices what he preaches. Elias has hit a home run with this book. It is a must for everyone, no matter where they are on the leadership scale."

— Tanya Unkovich, Author of *Unplanned Journey: A Triumph in Life and Death*

"When I first met Elias, it was obvious he was a man with strong values and a commitment to those he coaches. This book will give you the skills to be a great leader to gain the most from your team."

— Michelle Pascoe CSP, Speaker, Career & Business Educator, and Author of *The VIP Principle*

"One of the most challenging roles for a leader is to lead a voluntary organisation. In *Liberating Your Leadership Potential*, Elias Kanaris gives you the keys that can help you change self-limiting beliefs to successfully lead volunteers with influence."

— Jonathan Low, CSP PCC 2015-16 President Global Speakers Federation

"A priority of mine in broadcasting is always to start with what I know. What I know about Elias Kanaris is that he is not only lavishly passionate about the outcomes of great leadership but that he has a deep-seated care for the outcomes of people influenced by those leaders. Take passion, attention to detail, and Elias's embodied altruism, and this read will inspire you to rise willingly as you experience his pulse for greater leaders, greater leadership, and a greater life."

— John Peachey, Keynote Speaker, Broadcaster, Author, and Communicator

"Many authors report on topics from safe and secure vantage points. But once in a great while, an author emerges from a place of deep embodiment. Such words are forged and fashioned from rich experience and personal incarnation. Elias

Kanaris has written a masterpiece, fleshed out in his life and community a long time before. Read it and be inspired. Live it and be changed."

— Kary Oberbrunner, Author of *Day Job to Dream Job, The Deeper Path,* and *Your Secret Name*

"Elias has been a student of many styles of leadership for over a decade. If you are looking for tactical solutions with effective outcome, this is the book! Elias will lay out the nuts and bolts of Mr. Mandela's leadership."

— Sheri Griffin, Entreleadership Coach and Business Owner, Theatre Design Group

"In the years I've known Elias, he has been an inspiration! Through sharing both success and failure with humble transparency, he has taught me much, and challenged me to dream bigger and bolder dreams, and actively pursue them. My world is better for having a friend of his character and determination."

— Trudy Metzger, Founder of Faith Girls Unleashed & Generations Unleashed

"Elias Kanaris genuinely cares for people—a great start for any leader. Elias is also a great storyteller and the 'real' stories of how he and others have learned to conquer their mountains and become great leaders are right here in this book."

— Yvonne Godfrey, Founder of the MIOMO Programme, Speaker, and Author of *Networking with God* and *Parenting Yadults*

"I have worked alongside Elias for some time now and he truly understands leadership. This book will be a key component of your leadership toolbox that you can't do without. You will definitely 'Liberate your Leadership Potential' and take your leadership to great heights and powers of influence, when you read this book."

— Linda Guirey, 'The Mindset Manager',
Speaker, Trainer, Author, Artist

"If you are really serious about taking your leadership skills and abilities to the next level, then this book is for you. I have known Elias Kanaris for over twenty years, and his knowledge and experiences, which he shares in this book, are authentic and valuable. There are teachings in this book that will help put you in a great position to take on leadership roles you never thought you could. Enjoy!"

— Denis Gianoutsos, Executive Coach, Facilitator, Speaker
and Founder of The Global Leadership Coach

"Elias has brought together his experiences and knowledge and combined them with the wisdom of another great man, Nelson Mandela, to highlight the essentials of leadership and life. A great read. It's worth taking the time to reflect on the lessons and how they apply to your life."

— Karen Tui Boyes CSP, Speaker, Educator,
Creator, and Leader at Spectrum Education

"Applying skills and characteristics from a truly remarkable man who transformed a country, this powerful book instills guiding principles for leadership, and the inspiration to build a reputable business with loyal customers and dedicated employees."

— Susan Friedmann, CSP, International Bestselling Author of *Riches in Niches: How to Make it BIG in a Small Market*

"If you ask people, 'Who are some of the most admired personalities of the twentieth century?', Nelson Mandela's name is sure to be cited again and again—the attitude he adopted following twenty-seven years of incarceration borders on being superhuman. This is where Elias Kanaris' book does such a masterful job. Many of us who are familiar with Mandela's story will never sleep a night behind prison bars, yet Elias speaks of the reader's 'jail of self-limiting beliefs' and how we might be set free from inhibiting mind-sets. I count Elias as a friend, and respect him as a leader, and I have no hesitation recommending this tapestry of Mandela's lessons, Kanaris' own leadership journey, and the application of both to anyone in a role of influence—read and be set free!"

— Glen Sharkey, Trainer and Speaker
(NSANZ Trainer of the Year, 2015)

LIBERATING YOUR LEADERSHIP POTENTIAL

CHANGING SELF-LIMITING BELIEFS
TO LEAD YOUR TEAM, ORGANISATION,
OR COUNTRY WITH INFLUENCE

ELIAS KANARIS

Liberating Your Leadership Potential: Changing Self-Limiting Beliefs to Lead Your Team, Organisation, or Country with Influence

Published by:
Aviva Publishing
Lake Placid, NY
(518) 523-1320
www.AvivaPubs.com

Elias Kanaris
Phone: +64 9 280 4420
Email: info@EliasKanaris.com

www.LiberatingYourLeadershipPotential.com

ISBN: 978-1-943164-83-7
Library of Congress: 2016943815

Editor: Tyler Tichelaar/Superior Book Productions
Cover Designer and Interior Book Layout: Nicole Gabriel/Angel Dog Productions
Author Photo: Rory Laubscher/Firefly Photography

Every attempt has been made to source properly all quotes.

Printed in the United States of America

First Edition

2 4 6 8 10 12

DEDICATION

To my wife Kay Kanaris: You have believed in me even when I didn't have enough belief in myself. I want to thank you and publically acknowledge you for your support and sacrifices to help me establish myself in my business. Your faith in God has been an inspiration to me, as have your values. You are more of a leader than you care to admit. I love you. I am grateful for you. Thank you, Kay, for believing in me.

To my surrogate mother, Maureen Murfitt: I am so very thankful that God put you into my family's life. You have become an integral part of my family, and I am grateful for your energy and support. You have shown me what it means to be a prayer warrior, and I pray for God's richest blessing over you and your family.

To my children: I am so proud of all four of you. You have shown me compassion and have allowed me to influence your lives in ways I had not anticipated. Thank you for allowing me to learn more about myself and for not judging me.

To my father and mother, Anastas and Mary Kanaris: Your leadership influenced me more than I care to think. You supported me financially and emotionally through my highs and lows. I thank you and look forward to reuniting with you in heaven.

ACKNOWLEDGEMENTS

No book is written alone so I would like to thank the many people who have influenced me in my journey:

Sir Alex Ferguson, Anastas Kanaris, Antoine de Saint-Exupéry, Arnold H. Glasow, Arsene Wenger, Arthur H. Miller, President Bill Clinton, Pastor Bev Mortlock, Bob Burg, Bob Marley, Booker T. Washington, C. Joybell C., Captain Bollard, Charlie 'Tremendous' Jones, Christian T.J. Simpson, Clive and Helen Ellis, Dale Carnegie, David J. Schwartz, Des Hague, Dick and Maurice McDonald, Gabriella Kanaris, Gary Chapman, Gary Hoogvliet, George W. Crane, Glenda Leonard, Harper Lee, Harry Petit, Helen Keller, Ian Wishart, Jack Welch, Jennifer Shakeel, Pastor Jentezen Franklin, Jesus Christ, Jim Collins, Jim Dornan, Jim Rohn, Joan of Arc, Joel Osteen, John Acuff, John Dewey, Dr. John C. Maxwell, Kary Oberbrunner, Kay Kanaris, Lou Holtz, Lance Armstrong, Mahatma Gandhi, Madeleine Kanaris, Mark Ogden, Marla Cilley, Mary Kanaris, Dr Masaru Emoto, Mona Yunan, Monti Bloom, Nancy Dornan, Natasha Gagarin, Nelson Mandela, Paul Adams, Paul Martinelli, Pastor Paul Scanlon, Peter Bondra, Pastor Peter Mortlock, Ray Keller, Ray Kroc, Richie Lewis, Richard Branson, Sam Walton, Scott M. Fay, Sheri Griffin, Simon and Yvonne Godfrey, Stephen Covey, Stephen King, Syd Jones, Warren Buffett, and Zig Ziglar.

I would also like to thank three more people who were all very influential in making this project work. Tyler Tichelaar for his support and expertise in helping me to edit this manuscript. Without his talent, this book would still be a D- document. Nicole Gabriel, for her expertise in graphic design. You brought my vision of Nelson Mandela to life. And finally, Patrick Snow, for his enthusiasm and support as my publishing coach. You were my biggest cheerleader, and without your expertise, this book may never have been birthed.

CONTENTS

INTRODUCTION

This book is not the biography of Nelson Mandela. It is about taking your leadership skills to the next level where you can influence other leaders around you and empower them to lead your team, your organisation, or your country with influence. It is about helping you to apply Nelson Mandela's character traits and wisdom to lead more effectively.

The quality of your leadership has a direct effect on the value of your company's stock. It has been shown that a company with good leaders can increase company stock by 900 percent over a ten-year period. The flip side of the coin is that a company with a poor leader will only see a measly 74 percent increase across the same period. How does your leadership style affect the value of your stock, and what is the domino effect on your key people?

Maybe you think that leadership has no impact on those who surround you. A staggering 37 percent of employees have cited bad leadership as the main reason why they have left their jobs. Another 39 percent feel underappreciated at work, whilst 77 percent of employees stated that they would work harder if given more recognition!

Whether you have people who are a direct report to you or not, you are still a leader. Maybe you are surrounded by people who can impact the profitability of your business and your paycheque. Think about the top two or three things that frustrate you the most about what happens in your business. How many of them relate to individuals in either the way they behave or their attitude?

Maybe you can relate to the following questions:

- Are you frustrated by the people who surround you?
- Do you sometimes think you could do a better job than them?
- Are you irritated when waiting for others to complete a task, or when they hand something back to you that you have to redo it?
- Do you wish you could take more time off and enjoy yourself with your loved ones, but you fear that if you took too much time away from your business, you'd come back to an even bigger mess?
- Do you wish you could make more money to invest in the things that will help you grow your business, or better still, in the luxuries you believe you deserve?

If you related to any of those questions, I feel your pain. Fortunately, you're not alone.... I sat in the same seat as you not so long ago. When I was the general manager for a financial services company, I had the title, but I felt I was surrounded by individuals who were sent to torment me. Little did I know it was up to me to lead them to the point where they would make contributions that outperformed my imagination. What you have to know about me is that when I was in school, I was always at the bottom of my class. My teachers never had any faith in me. In fact, they believed I was likely to be in jail; they could never foresee that one day I would be breaking others out of the prisons of their limitations.

In this book, you will learn that:

- Everything rises and falls on leadership
- What you say has tremendous power on the outcome of your business
- Making a profit is good
- Developing relationships is easy
- Taking action is important
- You can improve your profitability by walking in your client's shoes
- By leading from the front, you can set the pace of your success
- You can reduce your headaches by surrounding yourself with people you can trust
- You can increase customer satisfaction when you do the right thing
- Your successes will be directly related to recruiting people with a good attitude
- Learning never stops and is your responsibility
- Allowing people to make mistakes is good for your business
- Your key people will stay loyal when you nurture relationships with them
- Your strength will come from overcoming obstacles
- Your biggest successes will come as a result of developing good daily habits

- You can get further, faster by planning ahead
- Encouraging your people is important
- You can get things done more easily by regularly rewarding good behaviour
- You can accomplish more by giving it over to God
- You can motivate and retain key people by including regular celebrations in your routine
- You can learn what not to do by avoiding examples of bad leadership
- Your life is on public display and even the slightest slip can become costly

If you apply the wisdom offered in this book, you will start liberating your leadership potential by jail-breaking your self-limiting beliefs to lead more effectively with influence.

Despite my disastrous academic record, I invested in my personal development and read many self-help books and inspirational autobiographies. One in particular, Nelson Mandela's *Long Walk to Freedom* impacted me more than many others. Whilst all of the books that I have read have helped me to change my personal outcome, I want to draw some lessons from Nelson Mandela's life that you can apply to your leadership journey.

Maybe, like me, you have been stuck in a jail of self-limiting beliefs. Maybe you have team members who are locked in that jail. Maybe you have aspirations to achieve more, but you simply cannot find the keys to unlock the doors that have imprisoned you. Maybe, like Mandela, you need to review your thinking and determine how it can affect your ambitions. In the introduction to his book, Mandela relates that President Clinton once asked him whether, after twenty-seven years in prison, he still hated his oppressors. Mandela admitted that as he walked away from prison, he was angry. He had been abused, lost his marriage, and lost the best years of his life. But then he had an epiphany: "I realised that when I went through that gate, if I still hated them, they would still have me. I wanted to be free. And so I let it go."

After reading these words, I let my insecurities and self-limiting beliefs go too. Maybe, like me, you can let yours go and accomplish more for your life, your business, your team, or even your country.

I have held senior roles in the financial services, information technology, and telecommunications sectors. I was the senior consultant in the largest telco here in New Zealand, working within a team responsible for the top twenty-four trans-Tasman customers with a combined billing of over $450 million per annum. I became the party president for a political party that contested the 2008 General Election in New Zealand, with overall responsibility for a 300+ strong volunteer workforce. As a founding partner of the John Maxwell Team, I was one of the first members invited to join the President's Advisory Council (P.A.C.), where I served for three years. I am the current national president for the National Speakers Association of New Zealand, and I am serving as the member at large on the executive committee of the Global Speakers Federation. I say all this not to impress you, but to impress upon you that if I can change, then so can you.

I can hear you moaning at me, "Not another self-help book! There's nothing new that Elias can tell me that I haven't heard before." The chances are that, like me, you have a stack of books on your bookshelf gathering dust, all promising you the elusive Holy Grail of leadership. People used to tell me that I wouldn't amount to much and that I was stupid, so the thought of improving myself was a remote fantasy. But I'm here to tell you that your past doesn't define your future. I want to encourage you to believe that you can change and start off with a clean sheet, using this book as the catalyst for your future self. Make this book your personal property, and use the blank sections I've left for you to write your thoughts down. Your interactive participation in completing the exercises in this book will dramatically improve your leadership capacity and retention of the material, both of which will impact your business and the key people who surround you.

I'm an executive coach, and I know the personal value that having a coach has had on my life. I'd like to coach you personally through your journey as you aspire to grow as a leader. Remember the last time you went on an airplane and sat through the safety briefing? What did the flight attendant tell you to do with the oxygen mask when it fell from the compartment above your head? Put it on the person sitting next to you? No—of course not! You were instructed to put it on yourself. Help yourself before you help those around you. As my mentor Dr. John C. Maxwell says, "Hi, my name's John, and I'm your friend!" I want you to think of me as your friend. We may not have met in person (yet), but by the time you finish reading this book, I hope you will feel as if you already know me. I will also give you access to some free resources to add even more value to your life. Just head to the Free Resources section at the end of this book for my recommended list of free resources that I believe will help you on your journey.

Are you ready to start liberating your leadership potential by jail-breaking your self-limiting beliefs to lead more effectively with influence? Now is the best time to start taking action. As I've said many times before, it's very hard to steer a parked car! Let's go!

"After one has been in prison, it is the small things that one appreciates: being able to take a walk whenever one wants, going into a shop and buying a newspaper, speaking or choosing to remain silent. The simple act of being able to control one's person."

— Nelson Mandela

Key #1

EVERYTHING RISES AND FALLS ON LEADERSHIP

"Before you are a leader, success is all about growing yourself. When you become a leader, success is all about growing others."

— Jack Welch

People think that leadership is about position or title. I beg to differ. Leadership is about what you are willing to do and how you can encourage those around you to do what they might not want to. In this book, you will discover a number of Keys to Leadership that are supported by experiences from my life and others that I have observed. Every success that you have accomplished in life is a direct result of leadership principles. You may not have thought of yourself as a leader or that you had accomplished much. That is where I found myself in 2008 as I transitioned out of the corporate world and (eventually) into my own business.

How Much of a Leader Are You?

Back in 2007, my life was really good. I had recently been

headhunted into a new role here in New Zealand. My pay-scale had increased over 30 percent, I was qualifying for bonus upon bonus, and through a number of activities that happened in parallel, I became debt-free. In the course of six short months, I had removed over $160,000 in debt!

I was the proud owner of my dream car, a Saab 9-3 Aero, and I was living the life of Riley. With valet parking at work, it was safe to say that I wasn't being pushed hard. I could arrive at work early (often getting in before 7am to beat the traffic), working through until 2pm and then heading off home in time to pick up the kids from school.

For the rest of the afternoon, my family and I would spend time together, enjoying life. I would prepare dinner and we would eat as a family.

By 8pm, we would tuck the kids up in bed; then my wife Kay and I would have some quality time together before I jumped back on my laptop around 9pm to finish off whatever work I had to do.

Despite this idyllic lifestyle, I had a burning thought that was festering in the back of my mind….

Towards the end of 2006, I had read a fascinating book called *Eve's Bite* by investigative journalist Ian Wishart. It is a well-researched, if somewhat dark, commentary on the influence of politicians on the culture and thinking within the New Zealand landscape. With a young family, living in an increasingly politically-correct country, I started to challenge my thinking on the status quo.

Having previously supported a member of my church to campaign in the 2005 General Election, I explored his ambitions for the forthcoming elections in 2008. It soon became apparent that we would both share a similar dream of affecting change in New Zealand.

What started off as an act of support towards the end of 2007 as we chartered and launched a new political party, grew into a seat on the party's board. I was enthusiastic, but politically naïve. My supporting role grew on a daily basis as I met regularly with other board members and we strategised the pathway forward for the election ahead.

One weekend, in April 2008, following a lot of discussion and prayer with Kay, I decided I wanted to dedicate a year of my time as a volunteer to support the party. As I attended our weekly Tuesday Board meeting, I approached our deputy leader, Paul Adams, and told him my plan. His response was truly underwhelming!

Not deterred, I repeated the same course of action with Richie Lewis, the party leader. Rather surprisingly, his reaction was similarly muted. Talk about a let-down....

The following day, I received a call from Adams, asking me whether I was serious about my offer. I confirmed that my position hadn't changed, so he invited me to a meeting on Thursday to discuss a role the party thought I might be suitable for.

When I arrived for our meeting, I was nervously anticipating that they would ask me to act as Adams' campaign manager. I started running through all the scenarios and questions that I wanted to ask them prior to taking on the role. I had significant doubts about my ability to undertake the role, with my having no prior political experience looming front and centre in my mind.

Nothing I had contemplated during my forty-five-minute drive, however, could prepare me for what happened. Instead of being asked to be Adams' campaign manager, they asked me to step into the role of party president. I was speechless!

I knew and respected Adams and Lewis well enough to understand that they had more faith in me than I did in myself! Without hesitation, I agreed to take on the role.

Again, I say this not to impress you, but to impress upon you that everything rises and falls on leadership. Leadership is not a title or position; it is the actions you take on a daily basis that determine the outcomes for you and those you lead.

When life throws you a curve ball, you better be ready to swing your bat and connect. And if you miss, you steady yourself and take another swing at the next ball pitched your way. If you take enough swings, you'll eventually hit the ball for a home run.

This was the first time in my life that I realised we all have a leader within us, waiting for the opportunity to emerge and claim the day.

What Would You Have Done in the Circumstances?

I would like to say that my experience in politics led to a happy-ever-after ending. But, unfortunately, it didn't. We did not manage to get any candidate elected, and I ended the campaign on a low. Physically and emotionally, I was drained. I had no choice but to regroup and to reset my priorities. The character of a good leader is not defined by how hard he or she falls, but by how resilient the leader is when setbacks occur. Let me back up a few years to give you some other examples of leadership.

It was an ordinary Tuesday, uneventful apart from a wardrobe malfunction.

As I got changed into my suit at my parent's house in Wimbledon, South London, I realised that I had not packed a tie! I was soon in the taxi and heading towards Heathrow Airport, where

I made a detour via the Tie Rack to pick up a new tie before I headed into the Business Club Lounge to await the boarding call.

With my new tie securely fastened, I took a leisurely stroll and proceeded to the departure gate where I was waved through to my seat at the head of the business class cabin.

The flight was UA929, heading to Chicago, where I was due to present at a conference.

The date was September 11, 2001.

Nothing could have prepared anyone for the tragedies that were about to unfold. Halfway through our flight, just after the crew cleared away our lunch, my world would be abruptly changed forever. I'm still unsure whether it was the panicked look on the faces of the crew as they scurried around the plane or the horrendous sound that I heard (I would later find out it was the sound of fuel being dumped from the plane in anticipation of our unplanned and premature landing), but we were soon reassured by Captain Bollard, who told us there was nothing wrong with the plane.

He went on to let us know that due to a "significant incident in the United States," all airspace had been closed. This resulted in our diversion to Gander Airport, Newfoundland, where we were one of thirty-nine planes grounded there as a result of the 9/11 terrorist attacks.

After a significant delay as the Canadians erected security, we were released from our plane some twenty-four hours after we had taken off from Heathrow. Following the completion of a thorough check of all our carry-on luggage, we were shuttled to the sleepy hollow of Gambo (population 2,000), where we became guests of the Salvation Army. Two hundred of my fel-low passengers entered the sanctuary and created makeshift sleeping arrangements on pews, across the floor, and eventually, on the army stretchers that were brought in as temporary beds for us.

What I hoped would be a short turnaround stretched into a five-day stay. Nobody had anticipated this arrangement, and two days into our stay, we were made aware that there was a funeral arranged for Friday afternoon.

No alternative option was available, so we had to come up with a plan to clean the church from top to bottom out of respect for the bereaving family.

That was when fellow airplane passenger Monti floated to the surface. He gathered us into the room and started to share his vision for how we could allocate the tasks to get the church tidied up and made ready for the funeral. He asked for individuals to put their hands up to take ownership of certain areas of the clean up, and soon he had about a dozen people (including myself) volunteering to get the job done.

Without his leadership, I dread to think what impact we would have had on the bereaving family. It is safe to say that during the funeral, nobody would have suspected that 200 stranded airline passengers were lurking in the church's depths. The deceased was given a dignified send-off and the event passed without incident.

Is Your Leadership Maturing with Age?

My personal journey into leadership was influenced by a decision I made as a young boy. In 1970, my family moved from Libya to London. It was a rude awakening for an eight-year-old boy. The hustle and bustle of England's capital city, combined with a significant change in temperature, confusing accents, and a distinct lack of beaches made it a challenging environment to grow up in.

My saving grace was the culmination of the world's oldest and most prestigious football ('soccer' if you're an American) knock out competition—The F.A. Cup—which came to a tumultuous head in May of 1971.

My elder brother had selected Liverpool as his team to cheer on; being the youngest boy in my family, I was given the 'left-overs', so I supported Arsenal in that historic cup final. Thus started my forty-five-plus years of loyalty with the one club.

If you are a follower of the English Premier League (EPL), you are aware that the most successful clubs have historically been Liverpool, Manchester United, and Arsenal, with the likes of Chelsea and Manchester City making recent inroads.

But when you measure the successes during the present era of the EPL (which was formed in 1992), Manchester United and Arsenal provide us with the history of the most successes and consistency throughout that period.

The common factor is that both clubs retained the same leadership over the longest period of time. Sir Alex Ferguson stood at the helm as Manager of Manchester United for twenty-seven years (1986–2013). His counterpart, Arsene Wenger, has led Arsenal since 1996, and at the time of this book going to press, still does.

After Sir Alex retired and handed the reins to his successor, Manchester United failed to qualify in the top four for the first time in over a decade. Arsenal, on the other hand, has broken the record with nineteen consecutive years of qualification to the prestigious UEFA Champions League.

What caused the dramatic fall from grace for one of the richest clubs in the world? All fingers pointed to Sir Alex's successor—David Moyes.

According to an article by Mark Ogden, "When he inherited a

squad of champions from Sir Alex Ferguson, Moyes resisted a swift clear-out and gave every player a chance to prove his worth, but his lack of a ruthless streak ultimately cost him dear, with many players failing to repay his faith."

The lesson we can learn here is that in leadership, you need to know how to read others.

It could be argued that Sir Alex had cultivated a strong relationship with his players, which was reflected in a level of loyalty and trust he could use to his advantage on the pitch. In his updated book *Alex Ferguson: My Autobiography*, Sir Alex identifies how his successor went against United traditions by adopting a slower playing style that, in his day, would not have been tolerated. He writes:

> The reason for playing at speed was that United players had been accustomed to operating that way," he writes. "If the tempo slowed for any reason, I would be into them at half-time. 'This is not us,' I would say. Playing with speed never hindered our results. It was our way: energy and determination in the last third of the pitch.

Knowing your people enables you to get the most out of them.

How Did the Daughter of a Peasant Lead France to Victory?

You may have studied, or at least heard of, a young girl who, at the tender age of sixteen, started to lead and unify the French army during the infamous Hundred Years' War. Her name was Joan of Arc, and she is known as the catalyst that helped her nation regain sovereignty from the English in the fifteenth century.

Joan indicated that it was around 1424, when she was twelve, that she began to experience visions that she described as both verbal communication as well as visible figures of saints and angels whom she could see and touch. Her own testimony as well as a royal document say that on at least two occasions, other people could see the same figures.

What is fascinating about her story is that a young teenager with courage was able to cast a vision of what could be done to change the fortunes of a war-torn country. Whilst her time on earth was short (she was burned at the stake in 1431 at the tender age of nineteen), her legacy lives on.

How Old Do You Have to Be to Become a Leader?

Irrespective of your age, I want to encourage you to understand that leadership has nothing to do with the mechanics of a chronometer. Upon graduating from university with my Master of Science degree in 1984, I joined the workforce in a full-time capacity. Aged twenty-two, I started my role as Electronic Test Engineer. It wasn't a glamorous role, but it provided me with an acceptable income stream that helped me to pay for my first car.

The timing of my appointment coincided with the promotion of my manager from Head of Electronic Test to Operations Manager. I was told to hang tight and to report to him until a replacement was found.

As it turned out, over the next six weeks, candidates rode a merry-go-round through the office door—unable to secure the role.

When I was approached about taking over as Head of Department, I was chuffed (that's English for honoured!). If the truth be told, I was quite cocky about being selected. But this turned out to be a baptism of fire.

It certainly proved that age wasn't a barrier to leadership roles, but my lack of leadership experience was compensated for by strong interpersonal skills.

Take the time to think through all the times when you were in a leadership role whilst in your younger days. Whether you captained a sports team at school, were a house prefect, or took office as a student leader, compile the list of your accomplishments. And no matter how small or insignificant the role was, take the time to document it in the space below.

LEADERSHIP ROLE	AGE

Applying lessons from Nelson Mandela's life:

Key #1 - EVERYTHING RISES AND FALLS ON LEADERSHIP

In his book, *Long Walk to Freedom*, Mandela talks about a visiting Methodist minister—Reverend Scheffer. Over time, as Reverend Scheffer became more familiar with Mandela and the other prisoners, he would poke fun at them. He accused the blacks of having it easy. The white man, Reverend Scheffer explained, had to find a solution to every problem. The blacks, on the other hand, he argued, always had an excuse. They would simply say, "Ngabelungu," which meant, "It is the whites."

Mandela went on to say, "He was saying that we could always blame all our troubles on the white man. His message was that we must also look within ourselves and become responsible for our actions—sentiments with which I wholeheartedly agreed."

As a leader, are you taking responsibility for your actions? Are you willing to live a life of blaming all of your troubles on others? Or are you willing to take action even if it means cutting off a part of you or your business for the good of the body? May I be bold enough to encourage you to take action around the area of your thinking and severing some of your self-limiting beliefs around yourself and your leadership capabilities.

Maybe by taking this action, you can start your journey along a new road....

"We pledge ourselves to liberate all our people from the continuing bondage of poverty, deprivation, suffering, gender and other discrimination."

— Nelson Mandela

Key #2

USING THE POWER OF THE SPOKEN WORD

"Be careful what you ask for—it may come true!"

— Anonymous

In Key #1, we saw that everything rises and falls on leadership. Leadership doesn't take into account your age, position, or title. But it can mature with age. Sometimes, you cannot appreciate your leadership capabilities, but that doesn't mean they don't exist. So, when it comes to your leadership, what are you saying about yourself or your capabilities? In this key, we will explore the power of the spoken word and how it can affect your leadership successes.

Why Should You Care What You Say?

As the marketing manager at Olivetti, I had the lead role working with our technology partner, British Telecom (BT). Since it was based in the UK, our subsidiary was the first to trial a new product that we were launching called the Personal Communications Computer (P.C.C.).

It didn't take me long to become fully conversant with the P.C.C., and I would often be brought in to demonstrate it to our customers.

After our in-country launch, we held a marketing seminar in our training centre in London to complete the international product launch. In the audience were all my peers from the other European subsidiaries—thirteen in total. No pressure! My task was to explain how the P.C.C. worked and how we would gain success in marketing the groundbreaking product.

I thought through our experiences and shared the findings, closing my presentation with a slide that simply said, "Demo, Demo, Demo!"

After everyone returned home, I thought no further about my presentation and carried on with the day-to-day activities demanded of me. Three months later, I was invited, at short notice, to attend another training day in our headquarters in Ivrea, Northern Italy. Once again, the P.C.C. was taking front stage in the meeting. Since I was asked to present again, I thought I'd review my previous slides. That's when I was reminded about my call to action.

When I arrived at the meeting, I was the last of six presenters tasked to give an update on our progress in marketing the P.C.C. to our local markets. To my surprise, four out of the other five presenters said, "Elias encouraged us to 'Demo, Demo, Demo!' That's exactly what we did and why we're so successful!"

Blow me down with a feather! I had *no* idea how powerful my words could be....

Why Should You Ignore the Names You Were Called When You Were Younger?

I grew up in an upper middle-class Greek family. My father, who was born in Jerusalem, moved to Libya via Jordan because of his banking career. He brought a great deal of banking experience to his new position in Libya, but he also imported much more.

A full-blooded Greek, he was a chauvinist who demanded respect within his own home. Please, don't get me wrong.... He was always a loving father. He just didn't know how to command respect through cooperation and connection. Therefore, he reverted to the only way that he knew—brute force and domination.

This translated to a barking command, which occasionally escalated into physical assertion, delivered via his leather belt. The recipients of his belt were my brother and sister. Fortunately, I was spared the belt—I had my mother to thank for that—but I was not spared his mental punishments.

Growing up, I was often called an 'idiot' by my father. As a young boy, this name-calling had a dramatic impact on my self-esteem and identity. What I didn't know was that my father called everybody an 'idiot'. He called the taxi driver an idiot, the dairy owner, heck, even the cat! I had no idea that he wasn't singling me out, and as a young boy, I didn't understand the impact that words could have on others.

Later in this book, I will detail how I ended up the 'dunce' in my class. I can confidently connect my father's name calling to my academic record. In 1998, I received the results of some psychometric tests that indicated I had the profile of a CEO and an exceptionally high I.Q. Therefore, I would like to explore the power that words have over us.

What Would Happen If You Asked for Something?

This summer it's been hot and humid here in Auckland, and

as a result, I've kept the windows and doors wide open to allow the breeze to cool me down. Unfortunately, as a result, we have had more than our fair share of flies!

It has become quite frustrating shooing them away. I tried to kill them using a fly swat, but the only damage I seemed to inflict was on the fly swat itself.

Frustrated by my lack of progress, I finally looked at one of those pesky flies as it sat on my coffee table, eye-to-eyes. It sat there indignantly ignoring me. By then, I'd had enough, so I decided to gain authority over my situation.

"Under the sound of my voice," I commanded the fly, "you will stay exactly where you are and I will kill you!"

I repeated this mantra over and over as I edged my way towards the fly. With my hands poised to clap a few centimetres above the fly, I waited until I felt the time was right. Holding my breath, I clapped my hand and instantaneously killed that fly!

I was over the moon with my accomplishment. One down... another dozen to go.

When I located the next fly, I repeated the exercise. I repeated my mantra and clapped my hands. Two out of two! I was on a roll.

Soon I discovered that I had eliminated flies number 3, 4, 5, and 6. Was there something in what I had created? Was there power in the words that escaped from my mouth?

How Excited Can You Get?

The spoken word, I have discovered, can be very powerful. When I was building my Amway business, I remember receiving a cassette tape that included a testimonial from a successful independent business owner, Ray Keller, who had built a business to the 'Diamond' level. It proved to be one of the most hilarious testimonials of Keller's journey to success in the Amway business.

Keller tells the story of attending his first Amway convention. He wasn't that interested in attending the event and was somewhat uncomfortable on the bus ride with a group of strangers who almost seemed to be in a euphoric cult-like state. But his attitude did a U-turn, and by the time he was on the bus heading back home, he was one of the first on the bus saying, "I'm excited! Are you excited?"

Needless to say, the euphoria of his first convention soon wore off. Keller and his wife Karla became embroiled in the mundane nature of their everyday lives, and his enthusiasm to build a business soon waned.

When we make a life-altering discovery, a period of improved activity drives us into the new reality of what our future might look like. But often, we then slip back into the older habits and start encountering the same old results.

What do we say to ourselves when that negative back-sliding occurs? Do we say things like, "I don't deserve that," or "It was too good to be true," or "I knew that would happen to me."

Take the time to think through some times in your life when you have accomplished something after you put your mind to it. It might have been a short-lived change, or something that lasted for a while, but eventually petered out. Write down the before and after scenario of what was happening and what changes you observed. Then write down what changes you made in your vocabulary that you can remember during that time. Was there a meditation or an affirmation that you had that was repeated over and over again?

EVENT	PRE-CHANGE STATE	POST-CHANGE STATE

AFFIRMATIONS CREATED

What If You Can't Remember It Word-for-Word?

In the late 1960s, I watched the TV series *Lassie*. You may have heard of it (or if you're as old as I am, you might have seen it!).

It featured a female Rough Collie dog named Lassie, who was the catalyst to solving mysteries and saving people who were in mortal danger. Often, Lassie would be bounding back to her master as she started barking.

"Woof, woof!" Lassie would bark.

"What's that, Lassie?" her master would reply. "Timmy's had an accident?"

"Woof, woof, woof!" Lassie would repeat.

"He's fallen down a well, and we have to save him?" her master translated.

"Woof, woof!" Lassie concluded.

And off they would go together to facilitate the rescue in time.

I think we should apply the 'Lassie Technique' to our lives. Think about it... "Woof, woof!" What does that mean? It appears that it could mean anything as long as it was said with enthusiasm!

If there is power in the words we use, then maybe we should be using our words more frequently. Maybe if you were to approach somebody, whether you wanted him to buy from you or to do something for you, you could start by crafting out the message, word for word, on paper. You could then practise repeating the words until you memorised them and they sounded convincing coming from your mouth.

But what if by the time you approached your target, you got all tongue-tied, and your words came out all wrong? What if all you were able to say was "Woof, woof!" but in an enthusiastic and compelling manner?

Your prospect would end up saying the equivalent of, "What's that, Elias? You want me to attend one of your Mastermind classes?"

"Woof, woof, woof!" you reply.

"And I need to pay you to attend?" he continues.

"Woof, woof!" you conclude.

"Absolutely!" your prospect says. "Where do I sign up?"

As silly as this appears, give it a go. Take some time right now to write down the script of what it is that you want to say to someone. Whether it is an employee, a supplier, or a prospective customer, write out the exact words you want to use when you're in front of them. And then practise, practise, practise.

So by the time you get in front of your prospect, you are so enthusiastic that the words just spill out of you. Even if you jumble up your words, they will still have a positive impact on the people you talk to. And when you add up all these points, you'll become excited and be able to 'Demo, Demo, Demo!'

WRITE THE SCRIPT FOR THAT IMPORTANT MEETING HERE...

Applying lessons from Nelson Mandela's life:

Key #2 - USING THE POWER OF THE SPOKEN WORD

Nelson Mandela practised as an attorney of law, joining in partnership with Oliver Tambo. He was working in a time when prejudice was rife, and as an African lawyer, he often fought contempt in the court system. Witnesses often refused to answer questions from a black attorney.

Yet Mandela knew that his only pathway to success within the court system was through the thoughtful use of words. He was self-confessed as being "rather flamboyant in court."

Mandela knew words could be chosen to create distractions or divert the course of justice. If a prisoner had died in police custody, often the coroner's verdict on the death certificate would read, "Death due to multiple causes" or some similarly vague explanation that would let the police officer off the hook.

Words are powerful. They can be used for good or for evil. Mandela used his words carefully. In his book, Mandela recalls the lengths to which he would go to articulate his message. Whilst incarcerated at Robben Island, the ANC (African National Council) formed its own internal organisation, called the

High Organ. Often, documentation and statements made by the ANC would go through the High Organ to ensure that the wording was acceptable.

As a leader, how much attention are you paying to the words you use. Are you carefully calculating the impact your words have on others, or are you just allowing your mouth to be a Gatling gun for the words that can wound those who surround you?

Today, modern technology brings voice recognition into our everyday lives. GPS systems can now be controlled by your voice commands. Choose your words carefully because they might end up directing your path to an undesirable location....

"Without language, one cannot talk to people and understand them; one cannot share their hopes and aspirations, grasp their history, appreciate their poetry, or savor their songs."

— Nelson Mandela

Key #3

MAKING A PROFIT IS GOOD

"Many receive advice, only the wise profit from it."

— Harper Lee

In Key #2, we explored the power of words in leadership. If I were to ask you to identify the main purpose for your organisation's existence, I'm sure I would receive a plethora of answers. You might say it is to provide a solution or service that solves a problem. Or to give great customer service. Or to help people to save money. These are all worthy outcomes of having a business, but I would suggest that the number one purpose of a business is to make a profit (or at least to cover its costs if it is a non-for-profit). In this key, I would like to explore with you why making a profit is good.

How Much of a Premium Will You Pay for Good Service?

When I was the general manager for a car leasing company back in the late 1990s, I came across an interesting phenomenon.

The reality of the situation surprised me to be honest.

Our service offering was simplistic. The client chose a vehicle that she wanted to drive. She determined how long she wanted the car—ranging from twelve to forty-eight months, with the most common being thirty-six.

Then she would choose an annual mileage. Let's say, for example, that she thought she would be travelling 15,000 kilometres (km) per year. So, over a thirty-six-month (three year) contract, she would expect to travel 45,000 km in total. The employees' job was to calculate a monthly lease rate that would allow the company to receive an income, own the car at the end of the lease period, and (hopefully) make a profit in the process.

The good news is that you don't need to be an accounting major to understand the mathematics behind the business model.

You get to purchase a vehicle at a fixed price from the dealer. Let's assume that the vehicle cost the company $10,000 to purchase. We would then crystal ball gaze and try to determine the value of the vehicle in three years' time, with 45,000 km on the clock. For this exercise, we estimated that its resale value would have depreciated to $2,800 by the time we came to sell it. Therefore, we needed to charge for the remaining balance of $7,800 over the three years. In the end, we would need to charge $200 per month for the lease (at a minimum) just to cover our costs.

The good news is that this is the end of the accounting lesson (phew I can hear you say!).

So let me put a small twist in this tale....

Picture the scene we encountered.

As the leading lease company in the country, we were servicing the biggest corporates. It would be quite common for them to approach us with a request to lease a number of identical vehicles at the same time. For example, we might be asked to purchase ten Toyota Corollas, which had a side benefit. When we purchased in bulk, we would end up getting a volume related discount from our supplier! This meant that we could either reduce our leasing cost or make more profit on each vehicle.

One day when I was speaking to my purchasing manager, he told me he had just placed an order with the dealer for eleven vehicles. It was one more than I was expecting, so I sought some clarity on the situation. It turned out that our largest client needed ten Corollas, but in addition to that, we had received an enquiry from a solo-preneur—let's call her Josephine Accountant—for exactly the same model vehicle. She ran her own practice, and she was looking to lease a vehicle on the same terms as our largest client.

The good news, from our perspective, was that we would now receive an even bigger discount from our supplier.

So when it came to calculating the lease price per vehicle, whom do you think received the cheaper monthly lease price?

If you said emphatically, "Your largest client!" you'd think that the answer was simple. Right?

Wrong! The answer was that Josephine Accountant received the 'cheaper' deal.

"How could that be?" your curious mind enquires.

The answer is a lot simpler than you would imagine....

When our largest client ordered its vehicles, it was looking for a high level of service. It expected its vehicles would be regularly serviced. We took the time to organise that for the client. We would contact its local dealer and book the car in for a service. We would organise for a loan vehicle to be made available. And we phoned up our client to give it the details in advance—including a courtesy call the night before the vehicle was due for its service.

Josephine Accountant, on the other hand, had to get that organised for herself.

Our largest client had a team of customer service reps available 24 x 7, answering calls within three rings to handle any enquiry or issue that occurred. If a driver had an accident outside of business hours, he or she could call the company's dedicated phone number in the middle of the night and our team took care of all the driver's needs. We would call out a tow truck, arrange a replacement vehicle, and book the damaged vehicle into the panel shop. No issue was too difficult for our experienced team to deal with. And our clients had a hassle-free experience as a result.

Josephine Accountant had to wait until the next business day to get the ball rolling on her accident claim. She had to pay for the tow truck, replacement vehicle, and (often) the cost of the repair.

Why does this happen?

Let me introduce you to the world of the trusted advisor.

In the world of sales, there tends to be two extremes.

On one end of the spectrum is the commodity supplier. It is easy to identify and tends to sell based on price. The most obvious commodity suppliers in your local market are often mobile phone companies. They all offer similar products and services and try to attract customers on the basis of the lowest price. In New Zealand, we have seen a proliferation of suppliers, like 'Skinny', emerge in the last couple of years.

Whilst their price points are low, they have to work hard to attract their clients. The downside is the high churn as they lose as many clients to their competitors as they seem to attract.

When you lead with price, the likelihood is that your clients will shop around, so the concept of loyalty becomes a thing of the past, and profits are paper thin. The business model is subject to volume. And fluctuations make it challenging to innovate and maintain pace with the competition.

In the case of car leasing, Josephine Accountant was a typical buyer who was motivated by price. Her decision-making process was heavily skewed towards fitting it into her (modest) budgets. She would shop around until she found the 'best price'. For our company to sell to her, we had to meet the market rates.

But to meet the rates, something had to give—in this case, it was service.

The other extreme on the scale is the trusted advisor.

In this role, the focus is on serving the client and adding value to the transaction. A trusted advisor will be focused on understanding his or her client's long-term business goals, and providing the services worth paying a premium for.

This focus translates to client loyalty, healthy profits, and raving fans.

As a leader, I want you to understand and embrace this Key: "Making A Profit Is Good". If you can articulate this philosophy within your organisation, you will stay in business.

How Much Value Add Are You Offering?

Back in 2000, I joined a company named SITEL. It was an outsource contact centre provider. Our main client in New Zealand was Telecom New Zealand. We were engaged to run and operate its directory service and front-line emergency service call handling.

By the time I was recruited, we had been delivering the service for nearly two years.

My role was that of product development manager. I was tasked to ensure that we could measure our performance on a global basis and draw upon our international experience—to look at ways that we could improve productivity and increase customer satisfaction. I was to review similar facilities within our group and identify their best practices to bring back to our operations. After all, the company employed in excess of 25,000 staff in a variety of contact centres across the globe.

However, I needed to address one small issue—we didn't have any other operations around the world that provided directory assistance services!

As a leader, it was my responsibility to find solutions—not fall back on excuses.

If you were faced with this issue, where would you start?

To me, the obvious starting point was to engage with two groups:

1) My client

2) My team

I needed to start asking questions to determine which issues we needed to solve. I had to understand what the current baseline was and then determine the end goal. If you have read Stephen Covey's book, *The 7 Habits of Highly Effective People*, you know that one of the main principles Covey works off is the principle of 'Start with the end in mind'.

My questions were formed to gain an understanding of the pain points and the desired outcomes. This process helped me to paint a picture of the landscape, but more importantly, it helped me to gain insight into the thinking of two camps.

Mapping the answers to those questions against our contract, it became obvious that I would need to help guide our team towards initiatives that could improve productivity and ensure that our client could afford to pay for a service that received limited revenues.

The goal for both organisations—Telecom New Zealand and SITEL—was to run a profitable business. It was the first time I came across a contract that respected that both parties needed to acknowledge that delivering a service on price alone was not going to provide a win-win.

SITEL was obliged to provide full disclosure on its accounts so Telecom could see it was receiving a service that wasn't overpriced. And the definition of that measurement was determined by the amount of profit SITEL made.

In too many instances, I have observed individuals and organisations focussed on cost-reduction. They would look at their supply chain management and endeavour to negotiate with their suppliers to get them to supply at the lowest price points possible.

This is a risky strategy. It encourages commodity supply mentality. Often competing suppliers would be sent into combat, pencils sharpened to determine who could undercut the other. Sometimes, the winning supplier would view the client for the prestige it offered, and it wasn't uncommon for the supplier to provide its services at a loss.

But whichever way your accountant looks at it, a loss is a loss, and the longer you deliver your service at a loss, the quicker you will go out of business.

Businesses have two objectives: 1) to make a profit (the primary purpose), and 2) to deliver a service that meets or exceeds the client's requirement.

As a leader, where is your focus in relation to the billing you have with your clients? Are you willing to open the bonnet to let the client take a look at the engine? Are you willing to operate under a full disclosure model?

The essence of a great relationship is trust. Leaders need to model building trust with their clients, and that starts with courageous conversations. Take some time now to review your current client relationships and ask yourself whether they are profitable. Once you have determined that, list the top three objectives your client has and check whether your products or services match them.

Then determine the top three objectives for your organisation and ask yourself whether the clients you have identified help you to accomplish them. If there is a disconnect, may I be bold enough to encourage you to go back to the drawing board? You may need to have a deep and meaningful conversation within your own organisation to determine the true value of that relationship. And then, bring your leadership strengths to the fore. Initiate the conversations that will help you grow the relationships that can lead to a billing review with your clients and, ultimately, more profitability for your organisation. After all, your clients will need you to stay in business so they can have continuity of service. Again, a win-win.

TOP THREE OBJECTIVES FOR YOUR ORGANISATION
1.
2.
3.

CLIENT NAME	MATCHES OBJECTIVE	REQUIRES ACTION

Are You Allowing People to Undervalue You?

If you own your business, or you have been involved in setting up a business, you know that the struggle to obtain clients at the start can be quite frustrating. It is often said that we overestimate what we can achieve in the short-term and we underestimate what we achieve in the long-term.

Having exited a successful career in the corporate world, I thought it would be easy for me to transition into my own business. Boy, was I wrong!

Acquiring clients had to be the hardest thing I did. For the most part, I thought I had a lot of experience to bring to the table. My strategy was simple enough...take everything I had learned in my career and life to that point and pack it into eighty hours, consisting of twenty sessions of four hours each, that I could shove down my client's throat over a ten-month period. Simple, right!

My graphic designer created my flyer, and then I went around speaking to the 'usual suspects'. You know the ones I mean. People with whom I had a strong relationship; the people I felt I could strong-arm into coming in and joining me; the people who were like me, either repositioning themselves in a new venture or not making much money! What a great strategy!

The investment was positioned at $200 per session, which worked out to a reasonable $50 per hour. Considering the content I was delivering, it was a bargain! I figured out that if I had a dozen people attending this program, I would be billing $4,800 per month—enough revenue to keep the wolf away from the door.

My overheads were minimal because I would be running this program in my living room out of my house. I already had the material created. All I needed was to structure it and format the handouts, and if I printed it in-house, I would keep my costs to a minimum.

However, two challenges arose that I had not anticipated as I started to market myself:

1. I had no proven track record.
2. My prospects had no money!

Hardly anyone was willing to pay to attend this program. Having run out of benefits they would receive by attending, I changed my tactic and tried other strategies to get anybody to attend. To entice people to join, I offered a number of incentives. As most of them failed, I resorted to bribery and corruption. I told them they could come for free and I would feed them!

Needless to say, that last strategy worked a treat.

But it didn't take long to realise that people were being fed, but seemed to leave hungry.

I wanted my delegates to learn leadership principles, and to go home and undertake some exercises to reinforce them. But often when they returned, few had completed their assignments. It became a challenge to overcome the awkward silence at the start of every session.

Before long, people started to come late and miss the occasional session.

John Acuff challenges modern thinking by asking, "Should you give away your dream for free?"

His argument is based on the principle that people don't value things that don't have value.

"Popular rhetoric will argue that it should be free," says Acuff. "That if you want a lot of people to get excited about it you should give it away much like the Red Hot Chili Peppers. That makes sense in theory. It would seem that if something cost $10 and something else was free, the free item would be more popular. More people, realizing they don't have $10, will jump on board with the option that costs zero dollars."

He goes on to explain that when he hosts free meetup events, only 30 percent of registered delegates turn up compared to 90 percent of attendees at his paid events.

We all want to add value to our clients. But there are times when you are giving it all away—some would say 'throwing the baby out with the bathwater'. If you sustain that practice, you will soon go bankrupt and be out of business.

As a leader, you need to understand that profit is your friend. If you offer a service that adds value to your clients, they will be more willing to stick with you. Go a step further and anticipate their problems, show them a solution that solves the issues, and speak their language, and you have a winning formula.

History has proven that people are willing to pay a premium for a service that resolves issues. As a leader, you need to have the vision to understand what your clients are going through. To borrow an idea from my good friend and coach Patrick Snow's book *Creating Your Own Destiny*, take the time to walk in your client's shoes.

A strong leader will make sacrifices to find out more about his (or her) clients. He will be willing to get his hands dirty by experiencing exactly what his clients experience. One of the best examples of this is the popular TV series, *Undercover Boss*.

In case you haven't seen an episode, the premise of the program is that the CEO of a company offers to work 'undercover' within his or her own business. The boss goes to elaborate lengths to disguise himself and a TV crew films the experience. The employees are told that the CEO is a contestant in a reality TV program and the prize is the seed money to start his own business.

This premise creates the ideal cover for the boss to receive first-hand insights to identify areas where change is needed within the business.

As a leader, what are you willing to do to find out what is working and what is broken within your business? How can you find out exactly what your clients need? When can you take time out to find out what your clients will be willing to pay a premium for?

The next time you sit with your accountant, take the time to ask yourself, "What is the #1 service that I can offer my clients that they will pay a premium for?" Until you are willing to value your clients, remember that people don't value things that don't have value.

Applying lessons from Nelson Mandela's life:

Key #3 - MAKING A PROFIT IS GOOD

In 1943, Mandela was part of a delegation that went to see Dr Xuma, the head of the ANC at the time. The delegation wanted to propose the formation of the Youth League. It was said that Dr Xuma had performed a great service to the ANC, having roused it from its slumber.

At the start of Dr Xuma's presidency, the ANC had 17s. 6d. (17 shillings and 6 pence) in its treasury. Under Dr Xuma's leadership, it had increased to £4,000. Unfortunately, Dr Xuma felt threatened by the delegates' proposal and tried to dissuade them from forming the Youth League as a highly structured group.

Despite Dr Xuma's objections, Mandela and his colleagues pursued their proposal and set up the Youth League. They understood their fellow countrymen's needs. They had reaffirmed and underscored the original concerns that formed the constitution of the ANC in 1912. African nationalism was their cry. Their creed was the creation of one nation out of many tribes, the overthrow of white supremacy, and the establishment of a truly democratic form of government.

Their manifesto stated: "We believe that the national liberation of Africans will be achieved by Africans themselves.... The Congress Youth League must be the brains-trust and power-station of the spirit of African nationalism."

By understanding the Africans' needs and articulating them in a manner they could understand, Mandela helped to add value to the people the Youth League would serve. Africans would be willing to pay 'over the odds' to join the Youth League, and soon the Indian community showed its support for the ANC protest. The Indians reminded Mandela and the Youth League that "the freedom struggle was not merely a question of making speeches, holding meetings, passing resolutions and sending delegations, but of meticulous organization, militant action and, above all, the willingness to suffer and sacrifice."

This is the action of a trusted advisor. Going the extra mile to show what can be done. As a leader, are you willing to take this path and show your team, your followers, or your clients what you will do to add value for them...?

"Money won't create success, the freedom to make it will."

— Nelson Mandela

Key #4

DEVELOPING RELATIONSHIPS IS EASY

"You can talk with someone for years, everyday, and still, it won't mean as much as what you can have when you sit in front of someone, not saying a word, yet you feel that person with your heart, you feel like you have known the person for forever.... Connections are made with the heart, not the tongue."

— C. JoyBell C.

Now that we have determined that making a profit is good, let us explore how we can make a profit in our business. Traditionally, a profit is made after the sale is completed. And people will buy from you when they get to know, like, and trust you. This key will explore the principles you can implement to help you develop relationships. It will also enable you to understand how you can leverage these principles inside your organisation.

Are You Creating Relationships or Creating a Mess?

When I was a senior consultant, my responsibility was to attend a meeting with our corporate clients and establish the status quo.

It wasn't too long before I discovered a recurring pattern with each client.

No sooner had I arrived to the meetings than the clients would start to 'throw up' all over me! They would complain about their issues and list the series of broken promises the last account manager had created. In fact, I joked to my boss that it might be cheaper for him to buy me some of those disposable jump suits that painters use. You know the ones I'm talking about...an all-in-one suit, with a zip up the middle and a hoodie. I argued that it would cost us less for me to take that off once the client had finished throwing up on me and chuck it into the bin, than it would cost for me to take my suit to the dry-cleaners!

The reality was that my colleagues had entered that organisation before me with one thing in mind—they were there only to hunt after the immediate sale. They would close the sale, collect the commission cheque, and walk away.

What is your current pattern of behaviour with the people you interact with? Are you being short-sighted and looking for the immediate gain, or do you treat every relationship as a long-term connection that's worth cultivating and nurturing?

Some level of joy is always derived from the immediacy of a sale or an outcome that is in your favour. But there's a bitter after-taste left in the customer's mouth if he perceives that you have just used him for your personal gain.

Are You Expecting Your Influence to Be Instantaneous?

I was privileged to be mentored by an incredible individual. His name was Jim Dornan, and he headed up an international organisation called Network 21 with his wife Nancy. Despite the most difficult personal circumstances (their son Eric was born with severe birth defects), they built one of the most successful businesses in the Amway world.

The Dornans set up a support system called Network 21 to help independent business owners like me succeed. Despite over thirty years in sales and marketing roles across a number of organisations in the UK and New Zealand, I still credit the teachings supplied by Network 21 as the most influential in my extensive sales career and as invaluable to my successes.

In particular, Jim Dornan opened my eyes to the true meaning of relationships. His view was always long-term and he embodied the significance of connections. In the book he co-authored with John Maxwell, *Becoming a Person of Influence*, there's a quote that I believe sums up this philosophy perfectly: "Influence doesn't come to us instantaneously. It grows in stages."

We live in a modern, microwave society, where we are expecting instantaneous results. Unfortunately, relationships require old-fashioned crock-potting. They have to mellow and mature over time to get the best flavours out of the dish.

Something that caught my attention early on was the way Dornan took time to connect with his audience. He would often encourage us to look at the person we were talking about from that person's perspective. The number of times his conversation was based on making his audience the centre of attention are too numerous to count.

He would encourage you to take an active interest in the other individual. For example, if you visited someone's house, you were encouraged to look for personal effects you could use as a bridge to connect with him or her. If you happened to see paintings of yachts dotted on the walls, chances were the person had a passion for sailing. Or if you saw a set of bowling trophies on the mantelpiece, then somebody within the household enjoyed 10-Pin Bowling.

What signals are you acting upon from the myriad of clues that surround you on a daily basis?

When it comes to leading others, I encourage you to follow the F.O.R.M. formula. It involves you asking your followers open-ended questions about the following four topics:

- Family
- Occupation
- Recreation
- Motivation

If you follow this formula, you can start to find out much more about someone. What is the person's family status? Is he married? Does she have children? What are the names of his or her spouse and children?

You can find out more about someone's occupation and how engaged he is within his roles. What drives him and what frustrates him? What are his ambitions and aspirations?

In terms of recreation, what does she do to unwind? Are there areas of commonality for you to use to help you build a stronger relationship? Do you follow the same sports, the same teams, or (even better still) do you support bitter rivals?

Finally, you are encouraged to explore what motivates people to carry on! When he finds himself with his back against the wall, what has to happen to encourage him to carry on? Having an intimate knowledge of this can become one of the most powerful ways of putting up the incentive to keep someone going when you need him or her to get to the next level. Dwight D. Eisenhower put it eloquently when he said, "Leadership is the art of getting someone else to do something you want done because he wants to do it."

I want you to list the top five most influential people in your company, or people who surround you if you are self-employed, and fill in the following matrix of information about them. This is a quick test for you on how well you know others and whether you have built deep relationships or whether they are superficial.

NAME	FAMILY	OCCUPATION	RECREATION	MOTIVATION	DEPTH OF RELATIONSHIP

Whom Are You Selling to?

When asked the question, "Are you a salesperson?" the majority of people reply that they're not in sales. According to Gallup, the majority of companies have removed the title "Sales Representative" from business cards, and rebranded their staff as "Consultants". Some of the more imaginative organisations now refer to their field staff as "financial advisers". Equipment salespeople are now "technical specialists". Many salespeople are referred to as "territory managers", or even "area vice presidents".

As a leader, do you consider yourself a salesperson?

One of the most effective sales techniques I've come across was demonstrated by a twelve-year-old girl. She came knocking on my door dressed in her Girl Guide uniform. She had a beaming smile on her face, a clipboard in one hand, and a basket in the other.

The first words out of her mouth were along the following lines....

"What a lovely day it is today. The sun is shining and it makes you look very radiant! Hi, my name is Marcie, and I'm a Girl Guide."

My opinion of Marcie was increased ten-fold by the mere fact that she had complimented me and used her upbeat and positive attitude to improve my day. Honestly, it could have been a cloudy day and pouring torrential rain, but whatever she said was bound to rub off on me.

"I'm here doing some market research," she said, "and I wonder if I can impose for five minutes on your busy and important schedule?"

Boy was she a pro! She knew how to butter me up, make me feel important, *and* she obtained my permission for interrupting my day. (Just think about that last point—I gave her permission to sell to me, and I felt I was in control of this relationship!)

The questions she started to ask me were related to basic demographics: the number of people in the household, adults and children, age groups, sporting interests, etc. Some questions were related to the busyness of our lives and the challenges of getting the kids ready in the morning. Others were related to the nutritional value of our eating habits. She was building up a great picture she was about to use as ammunition against me to persuade me to buy her cookies....

I was then offered some samples, which I was asked to grade on a scale of 1 to 5 (least to most enjoyable).

Well, I think you can guess what the last question was on her clipboard: "How many cookies would you like to order?"

Man was she good! Who would have thought that an innocent

twelve-year-old could be a ninja salesperson in disguise?

When you're in a leadership position, you're always selling to others. Ask yourself how you are doing in terms of creating and maintaining relationships. Friends buy from friends, and they often buy after they get to know, like, and trust you. Leadership follows the same principles. People will buy into your vision *after* they buy into you!

How Closely Are You Related to Each Other?

When I first arrived in New Zealand, I ended up spending a night in a Bed & Breakfast here in Auckland. In the morning, I joined a table for breakfast and started talking to the gentleman sitting to my right.

He was a filmmaker, visiting from Germany. He was creating a documentary on body art.

As we spoke, he made the following comment in his heavily-accented English. "Do you know vaz I like about zee Nuu Zealanderz? Vhen you pick zem up vhen zey are hitch-hicking, you become zee best of friendzz vizzin five minutes... Und, you find out zat you are related to each ozzer vizzin ten minutes!"

New Zealand must be one of the world's biggest villages. It is said that if you pass wind in the North Island, someone will smell it in the South Island!

Making friends is one of the most powerful things you can do as a leader. Relationships are the foundational building blocks to developing people around you and leading them. John Maxwell is well known for teaching on 'The Five Things That I Know About People'. Here is a summary of his teaching:

1. **Everybody wants to be somebody:** Isn't that true? I've yet

to meet somebody who wakes up in the morning and says, "I wonder if I can become a failure today!"

2. **People don't care how much you know until they know how much you care:** Another way I've heard John teach on this topic is through the statement, "You have to touch a heart before you ask for a hand!" If you want to touch people and change lives, you have to touch them relationally first. Don't impress them with your intellect; impress them with your compassion.

3. **Everybody needs somebody:** If you've ever heard someone say, "I'm a self-made man!" the chances are that they haven't made much! If you don't think you need anybody and that you can operate independently of others, then I'm here to burst your bubble. You can't achieve greatness by yourself. Even Sir Edmund Hillary needed the assistance of Sherpa Tenzing Norgay to conquer Mount Everest.

4. **Anybody who helps somebody influences a lot of somebodies:** If you influence a child, you affect a life; if you influence a father, you affect a family; if you influence a leader, you affect all those people who look to that leader. The power of influence always adds and multiplies.

5. **Today, somebody will rise up and become somebody:** How much value do you put on everybody that surrounds you—whether the person works for you, is in your social circles, or is a young upstart who is currently an 'ankle-biter'. Do you look at people and judge them on where you see their worth, or do you automatically place a 10 out of 10 on top of their heads? Maybe you can see their value before they see it themselves. This is an attribute of a great leader. Do you have it?

Applying lessons from Nelson Mandela's life:

Key #4 - DEVELOPING RELATIONSHIPS IS EASY

After the Rivonia Trial, where Mandela was found guilty of treason, he and his colleagues were sent to prison. That fateful day was Friday, 12 June, 1964 and thus started their life imprisonment. The following day, they were transported to the infamous Robben Island, which became Mandela's home for eighteen of his twenty-seven years of incarceration.

It soon became apparent that they were to receive no privileges. In fact, they had to endure a classification system: A, B, C, or D. The highest classification was A, and with it came the highest privileges; D was the lowest and conferred the least privileges. Mandela and the other political prisoners were automatically classified as D on admission. To make matters worse, it normally took years for a political prisoner to raise his status from D to C.

The prisoners despised this corrupt and demeaning classification system. With it came hardship, ranging from insubstantial meals to inadequate clothing. They even had to endure damp and cold cells that, coupled with malnutrition, led to considerable health issues.

Mandela speaks of the way he overcame some of these hardships. The warder in charge of their section became the most important person in the prisoners' lives. The warder was more important than the head of the prison, the commissioner of prisons, and even the minister of justice!

If you wanted an extra blanket, and petitioned for one, the commissioner of prisons might tell you it was against regulations. The minister of justice would provide no response, and the head of the prison would object that if he gave you one, then he'd have to give one to every prisoner.

Mandela stated: "But if you approach the warder in your corridor, and you are on good terms with him, he will simply go to the stockroom and fetch a blanket."

Mandela showed that developing good relations was important, and with the right motivation, it could be accomplished despite the adversarial relationships involved. As a leader, try using Mandela's techniques to open doors that lead away from the prison you find yourself in....

"People respond in accordance to how you relate to them. If you approach them on the basis of violence, that's how they'll react. But if you say, 'We want peace, we want stability,' we can then do a lot of things that will contribute towards the progress of our society."

— Nelson Mandela

Key #5

WALKING IN YOUR CLIENT'S SHOES

"Walking with a friend in the dark is better than walking alone in the light."

— Helen Keller

In this leadership journey, we have seen the importance of relationships and how they can impact your leadership. Key #5 will explore the importance of taking a deeper dive to understand your clients' needs. Often you will hear the term 'servant-hearted leadership' used to describe a type of leadership trait. I believe that by walking in someone else's shoes, you can learn more about that person's needs. Think of it as experiencing life from his or her viewpoint.

Are You Serving Others?

When I was growing up in Libya, my father insisted that my siblings and I had to serve others.

Put into practical terms, it meant that when we had visitors, we were told to take their coats and hang them up. We were to ask them what they wanted to drink, and we were given the task of preparing it and serving them. But my father didn't stop there. He even insisted that we should light up a cigarette before we passed it on to our guests!

Before you get up in arms, it was the 1960s and we were not as aware of the dangers of smoking. And thankfully, I didn't get addicted to smoking myself!

Why do I share this story with you? Because it didn't take too long before we knew that Uncle Andrew took a Scotch on the rocks (with four blocks of ice) and that Aunty Theresa would have an Ouzo with plenty of water but no ice.

Getting to know people can take many guises, but the benefits of knowing somebody and his or her likes and dislikes can lead to a deepening relationship. As Zig Ziglar said, "You can have everything in life you want if you help enough other people get what they want!"

I like to think that if you can step into somebody's shoes, you are more likely to get to know that person. And by knowing him, you can start to serve him. And by serving him, you can get him to do things for you.

That's the first level of influence you can have with others.

How Did El Chapo, One of Mexico's Leading Drug Lords, Manage to Escape Three Times from Various Maximum Security Prisons?

I'm known as *the* Jail-Breaker. This nickname provided a talking point when I attended the National Speakers Association conference recently.

In case you have not been following the international news, at the time this book went to press, Joaquin "El Chapo" Guzman had become the United States' most wanted man following his audacious escape from a high security prison. It is alleged that a $5 million tunnel was built under his cell over the twelve months prior to his escape. At least seven prison officers lost their jobs after his escape.

Local commentary indicated that the escape probably cost closer to $20 million, when you consider how many people may have been paid off for their services and involvement with it.

How does El Chapo's escape relate to growing leadership? Well, just like his hidden tunnel, there are five hidden leadership tips and tricks we can learn from this situation:

1. **Know your clients inside out:** I suspect El Chapo spent time researching the prison guards and other inmates who could help him execute his daring escape. He would have needed to know their motivations and understand the value they would provide in aiding with his escape.
2. **Don't underestimate the cost of building a relationship:** People are speculating that the overall cost for El Chapo to break out of prison could be as much as four times the cost of building the tunnel. What you have to remember is that for any significant long-term relationship, you will be undertaking a marathon—not a sprint! Take your time to nurture your relationships and remember that good things come to those who wait.
3. **Identify your 'Inside Man' (a.k.a. Key Stakeholders):** There's no doubt in my mind that El Chapo didn't break out of prison by himself. He needed help. Developing relationships is the same—you'll need help from the 'inside'. Chart out the key relationships you are trying to develop and ask yourself, "Whom do I know who is connected to the person I'm trying to develop a relationship with?"

4. **Ensure you are aligned with your team:** According to the *Wall Street Journal,* nearly fourteen months before El Chapo escaped from his maximum-security cell through a tunnel, one of his Sinaloa Cartel lieutenants broke out of another prison in the same way. Help your team members escape from their jails by gifting them copies of this book and taking time to implement the keys outlined here together.

5. **Don't leave any stone unturned:** It was reported in *TIME* that at least seven people had been arrested, including Librado Carmona Garcia, the head of the maximum security prison where El Chapo had been housed. Building relationships has to go up as well as down throughout an organisation. Make sure you are aware of the relationships people have within your team and with external influencers. The more you understand about others and their relationships, the better equipped you will be to identify potential stumbling blocks of political alliances that could hinder you.

So take a leaf out of El Chapo's book and ask yourself, "Have I understood all my key stakeholders, identified and neutralised my opponents, and am I willing to carry on with 'business-as-usual' until it is time to pull the trigger and go to the next phase?"

What Lessons Can Life Teach You?

In August 2013, I was lucky enough to invest two days with Scott M. Fay, the Vice President of the John Maxwell Team. During the two days we had together, Fay took me through my Lifeplan™.

The majority of our first morning together, Fay encouraged me to share stories about my life. In particular, he was looking for what he referred to as 'turning points'. For example, the birth of your first child is a turning point.

As I recalled my life, he took copious notes. By lunchtime, we placed a series of flip chart pads on the walls and started to document these turning points in chronological order. Over the course of the afternoon, we wrote out twenty individual turning points.

Each turning point would produce a turning point learning, which, in turn, delivered a message from my life. For example, a turning point for me came when I was thirty-three. It was the year I immigrated to New Zealand. Until that point in my life, I was swayed by other people's thinking. It influenced my actions and most of my decisions were made for me by others.

Analysing this change in my life taught me that when I had no external noises (i.e., the voices of my family and friends) to colour my thinking, I could make the right decisions for myself.

It is interesting that I needed to spend two days locked in a room with Fay to get him to unlock something I didn't know about myself. So here's a simple question for you to ponder: How well do you know yourself?

If you want to get to know others better, you have to start with knowing yourself!

Take a few minutes to map out your life and write down as many of your turning points as you can remember. Most people will identify thirteen to seventeen. Take your time with this exercise, but don't get all bent out of shape if you only come up with eleven or twelve.

TURNING POINT	AGE

Is What You Are Saying as Important as How You Are Saying It?

I used to work alongside a very capable chap who must have been one of the brightest people I ever knew. Unfortunately, he had a dreadful habit of alienating others.

He used to send out short emails, often limited to just a subject title—no content in the body of the email. Or he would get straight to the point and ask (some would say demand) that a certain task be undertaken.

He considered this technique efficient. The recipient often perceived it as rude!

What extra effort does it take to stop and think about the way you word an email or how you have a conversation with someone else?

When I write an email, I will often take the time to stop and think about the individual I am writing to and try to incorporate something personal in the opening paragraph. I might know that he or she has an elderly family member who has been unwell or a child who has achieved something of note. If it's appropriate, I will make sure I include a short comment that brings that topic to the forefront of our conversation.

The impact of this simple technique is that I have just taken a few moments to walk in my client's shoes.

People often feel a sense of connection with others because they feel that person has taken an interest in them. Connecting with people is often more than just words; tone and intent also make up a large part of the conversation. As my mentor John Maxwell often says, "People don't care how much you know until they know how much you care!"

Is What You Are Saying Being Misunderstood?

When I lived in the UK, I was sent on a public relations training program. It was a great experience to help me improve my skills when I was interviewed by the press.

We were encouraged to find out whom we were speaking with prior to commencing any conversation. That way you could identify whom the individual was and what media organisation he or she might work for. It was also meant to protect you from blurting out a 'state secret' that would end up on the front page of the tabloids the next day.

The next tip we were given was to ensure that we had three unique selling points (USPs) we could refer to. Those points would enable us to position our company and/or product in a positive way.

During the training, we had a role-play exercise. We were given a scenario where we would be meeting up with an individual who was going to interview us. We would be asked a series of questions and respond to them whilst our colleagues sat around and listened to our answers.

At the end of the role play, the following four things would happen:

1. We would report to our colleagues with a summary of the interview and how we thought it went.
2. We would identify the key points made and suggest a recommended headline for the article.
3. Our colleagues would give us their feedback on what they had heard and what they thought went well or could be improved.
4. The interviewer (a seasoned journalist) would then give us his take on the article he would be writing—inclusive of the headline.

One of my colleagues started his interview, which went along the following lines...

"I understand that the product you are launching is called IBIS," the journalist enquired.

"It was supposed to be IBIS, but we had to change the name to IBISIS," my colleague replied.

"Why was that?" asked the journalist.

"Because another Dutch company called their product IBIS, and we had no clue until it came out by accident. But it's all right," my colleague continued, "because I'm sure that the KLM plane that crashed into the apartment block in Amsterdam took out those Dutch b*st*rds!"

Without skipping a beat, he laughed out loud and continued the conversation with the journalist. It was a surreal moment.

The journalist showed no emotion and continued with the interview.

When they finished, my colleague was asked how he thought the interview went. He was very pleased, sharing the points he thought the journalist would focus on. On a scale of 1 to 10, he gave himself a solid 9 for his performance.

Our feedback painted a different picture. The insensitive nature of his comment was fed back to him, and we expressed our shock over it. Despite our observations, my colleague was in total denial.

The journalist closed off that session by telling us that his headline would read, "COMPANY PAYS FOR PLANE TO TAKE OUT ITS COMPETITORS." He then said he would quote my colleague as saying, "I hope that the KLM plane that crashed into the building took them out."

As a leader, your words are powerful, so you need to ensure you are using examples in context. Take the extra time to put yourself in your client's shoes and think through how he or she might interpret your comments.

Applying lessons from Nelson Mandela's life:

Key #5 - WALKING IN YOUR CLIENT'S SHOES

On the morning of December 5th, 1956, whilst still living in Johannesburg as a free man, Mandela was awoken by a loud knocking on his door. This led to his imprisonment at "the Johannesburg Prison, popularly known as the Fort, a bleak, castle-like structure located on a hill in the heart of the city."

By this stage, a total of 156 people had been imprisoned. They represented a cross-section of the community, with one hundred and five Africans, twenty-one Indians, twenty-three whites and seven coloureds. More importantly, they represented almost the entire executive leadership of the ANC.

During the two weeks the prisoners were there, their communal cell became a focal point for the once far-flung freedom fighters, allowing them the opportunity to have the largest and longest unbanned meeting of the Congress Alliance in years. Mandela observed: "Each day, we put together a programme of activities.... Talks on a variety of subjects were scheduled... (including) the singing (of) freedom songs."

These programmes includes the reciting of a praise song in honour of Shaka, the legendary Zulu warrior and king. Upon its conclusion, Chief Luthuli sprang to his feet and bellowed, "Ngu Shaka lowo!" ("That is Shaka!") and then proceeded to dance and chant. The whole congregation of prisoners joined in enthusiastically and emotionally. In that moment, there were no Xhosas or Zulus, no Indians or Africans, no rightists or leftists, no religious or political leaders. Mandela observed: "[W]e were all nationalists and patriots bound together by a love of our common history, our culture, our country and our people. In that moment we felt the hand of the great past that made us what we were and the power of the great cause that linked us all together."

The ability to walk in each other's shoes brought these men closer together. A bond was formed and strengthened. Their walk together became an integral part of their leadership growth....

"Know your enemy—and learn about his favourite sport."

— Nelson Mandela

Key #6

LEADING FROM THE FRONT

"It doesn't matter what everybody else is doing—be the change you wish to see in the world."

— Mahatma Gandhi

Seeing life from another person's perspective can be powerful. Allowing yourself to walk in someone else's shoes will empower you to observe the challenges he or she is facing. Now that you have gathered this information, what do you propose to do with it? Key #6 encourages you to be the change you want to see in this world. Stop talking about the issues; start doing something about them. Strong leaders will always be leading from the front!

What Do You Expect Others to Do to You?

I'm a man of faith. I make no apologies for that. However, I do not mean to force my faith down your throat. I would be untrue to myself and my faith if I didn't share the impact that faith has had on me and my leadership journey.

Instead of ignoring it, I'd like you to journey with me for a few moments. If you are by any way offended by my faith, may I suggest that you skip this section and read on? Otherwise, I'd like to welcome you into the following insight.

We all know the phrase, "Do unto others as you want them to do unto you." But where did it originate?

My first recollection of this phrase is when I was attending Sunday school at my church in Libya. In Matthew 7:12, Jesus says, "Do to others whatever you would like them to do to you. This is the essence of all that is taught in the law and the prophets."

Some people call this the 'Golden Rule'. I'd like to think of this as common sense. Unfortunately, as the coffee mug my wife bought me eloquently reminds me, 'Common Sense Isn't That Common'!

What is the opposite of the Golden Rule? I guess it would be the 'an eye for an eye, a tooth for a tooth' rule. Give unto others what they have given unto you. As an alternative, it sucks! What this rule is advocating is a retaliatory stand. Vengeance is Mine, says the Lord....

Mahatma Gandhi summed it all up when he said, "It doesn't matter what everybody else is doing—be the change you wish to see in the world."

I call this Key 'Leading From the Front'.

As a leader, it becomes your responsibility to set the pace, set the culture, and set the expectation. Who better than you to define the heartbeat of the organisation? They say that the fruit doesn't fall far from the tree. Do not expect your team to behave in a different manner from you.

Maybe you would think of this as 'monkey see, monkey do'. If you have children, it's like saying, "Do what I say, don't do what I do!" Children will mimic you. So will your team.

Do You Operate with a Servant Heart?

Jesus Christ is often lifted as the example of 'servant-hearted' leadership. I like to believe I have implemented this within my leadership style. This has not happened by accident, but as the result of experiencing it firsthand.

I am blessed to have family and friends dotted all over the world. Since my earliest recollections, I have always enjoyed my trips to the U.S. where I have a concentration of relatives. In particular, I have a cousin, Mona, who has shown me the true meaning of servant-hearted leadership.

Each time I planned a trip to the East Coast, she was the first one I reached out to. Her enthusiasm would flow over from the first WhatsApp message, to our voice-to-voice calls. She would be planning her schedule to coincide with mine.

If the opportunity arose, she would pick me up at the airport—irrespective of the time my plane arrived. During my stay, she would work from home to ensure she could help and serve me. She would complete tasks late at night or early in the morning to open up time for me.

If you were to think her hospitality was all about me, then you're wrong! She would set aside time like this for people who matter.

I've seen Mona take time to help prepare a meal, to clean the house, and to chauffeur people around. And it was always completed with a smile on her dial! I have gotten to know Mona quite well. She's an incredibly capable person, and she's accomplished a lot in her career, which has spanned twenty-four years in the pharmaceutical industry.

During that time, she has been under intense pressure to deliver projects by deadlines, encountered difficult people, and faced legislative guidelines that held multi-million dollar fines. But one thing has been constant throughout...her attitude.

Mona lives this Leadership Key of Leading from the Front better than most.

Are You Willing to Serve and Connect?

I had the pleasure to host Patrick Snow during his tour of New Zealand in 2016. Known as the Publishing Doctor, Snow is an international best-selling author, professional keynote speaker, and book marketing and speaking coach. He has been featured globally on radio and TV and as a cover story in *USA Today*, *The New York Times*, and *Forbes*.

His presentation style is infectious and engaging. He uses humour well, and he is willing to pour out his lifetime of knowledge to add value to his audience.

During his keynote presentation, he referenced how people buy from their friends. In fact, we all know that people will buy from you when they get to know, like, and trust you. Snow went on to say that most people in business tend to sell and market to their clients. Then he suggested a better alternative: 'Serve and Connect'.

This is an interesting concept. It is something Zig Ziglar's famous quote embodied: "You can have everything in life you want if you help enough other people get what they want!"

I like what Ziglar is encouraging us to do. By taking the viewpoint of leading the change, you can add value to others. When you add enough value to others, it will be returned to you, pressed down, shaken together, and flowing over.

In an increasingly self-centred world, we need to start making the change we want to see in this world. Leadership starts with leading yourself. As I mentioned in my introduction, when you see the safety demonstration on the plane, you are encouraged to put the oxygen mask on yourself first before you help others.

What are you willing to do to strengthen yourself? Are you investing in a coach? Do you attend conferences to educate yourself and network with other leaders? Have you read an autobiography of a famous international leader you can learn from?

As a leader, I had to go through difficult growth phases where I learnt from my mistakes. Some of them were painful, occasionally costing me in financial as well as emotional terms. I thought that as a leader, I just needed to be strong and take the world on my shoulders. That belief proved to be a mistake.

My personal breakthrough came after I joined the John Maxwell Team (JMT). There I met a number of like-minded, strong leaders who wanted to change the world. We were encouraged to take the oxygen mask and apply it to ourselves before we tried to help others. One lane we could choose to travel in was the coaching lane. Our head of faculty leading this lane was Christian T.J. Simpson. He encouraged us to form coaching partnerships, and it was in one of those partnerships that I experienced one of my defining moments.

I partnered up with Sheri Griffin, another founding member of the JMT whom I had met for the first time over lunch at our certification program in West Palm Beach back in August 2011. We had quickly bonded and shared many aspirations and dreams. Although geography separated us (Griffin lived in Austin, Texas while I lived in Auckland, New Zealand), we managed to arrange regular coaching calls. For one call, I would coach her, and on the alternate call, she would coach me.

The purpose of coaching is to be in a relationship with someone who holds you accountable to your dreams and aspirations. It is a relationship with an individual who is often more committed to what you want to achieve in life than you are! Someone who has no agenda other than your growth and success.

The best coach is someone who is asking open, explorative

questions and listening deeply to your answers.

Through my coach, I was able to explore how my role as a leader was not to drag people behind me, or worse still, to go on that journey to the top of the mountain by myself. It was to learn that I needed to lead from the front, but that I also needed to grow myself to allow people to help me lead. If I didn't change myself, then I could never fulfil my dream of 'positively impacting one million households around the world'!

Where Do You Look for Leadership?

In Key #1, I referenced some of my experiences when I ended up as the guest of the Salvation Army in Gambo, Newfoundland. I arrived there after my flight, UA929, was diverted from its destination of Chicago as the result of the 9/11 terrorist attacks.

For those of us who were travelling that day, it became a chaotic and unsettling time. We had no indication of the issues that had led to our diversion, and as we landed on the tarmac at Gander Airport, we were one of thirty-nine planes that parked on the extensive airfield.

We were initially alerted to the issue by an announcement from Captain Bollard. His calm voice of authority helped us to accept our fate, and we immediately knew we were in safe hands. Upon landing, he was able to share more about the tragic incidents that had transpired at the Twin Towers in New York City.

He shared as much information as he had received and proceeded to let us know that he would be piping in the BBC World Service to enable us to get up to speed. For the remainder of the twenty-four hours since our departure from London Heathrow until we were sanctioned to disembark, our newsfeed was courtesy of the BBC and Captain Bollard's foresight.

We were eventually transported to the Salvation Army Church in Gambo, where we settled in for a further four days. But the information flow did not stop when we stepped off the plane. Every day, Captain Bollard and his Purser Natasha Gagarin came to see us and gave us an update on progress being made. They were able to inform us on the process that United Airlines was going through in Chicago. We were allowed to ask questions, and Captain Bollard and Purser Gagarin provided as much information as they had access to.

The sense of relief was palpable. During a time of uncertainty, Captain Bollard delivered leadership that personified the opposite of the damage that terrorism created. He was able to let us know the issues they were dealing with. He covered the steps they took to prepare the plane and let us know that when we returned to the airport, certain passengers would be segregated for further enquiries. It transpired that the background checks completed by United Airlines on the passengers had pulled up a couple of anomalies.

Some leaders would choose to keep their people in the dark. Captain Bollard offered us full disclosure. He didn't try to make things up. Instead, he preferred to draw the line at answers he could competently talk about. He was unwilling to fabricate answers just to have something to say.

To this day, I am grateful for his leadership and the lessons we learned despite the tragedy that 9/11 epitomised.

When Was the Last Time You Apologised to Someone?

I wish I had learned the lessons on good leadership that Captain Bollard demonstrated to us in 2001. I was general manager for a car leasing company in 1998, responsible for a $160 million asset portfolio, where I ran the company's sales and marketing divisions. We were the market leader in New Zealand at the time.

In my mid-thirties, I thought I knew it all. I was appointed to a senior role. I had the title; therefore, I thought I had the authority. How wrong I was! What I had is often referred to as 'Positional' Leadership. It is the lowest rung on the ladder. Irrespective of your previous experiences, when you join another company, you always start on the lowest rung of the leadership ladder. You have to establish yourself and build up to your previously held leadership level.

John Maxwell suggests that you can't lead people until you like people. He calls that the 'Permission' level of leadership. This is the second level on the ladder.

At that point in my leadership life, it might be true to say that I probably didn't even like myself, let alone others. I remember having clashes with my marketing manager. We butted heads like rams fighting for the affection of a ewe.

The truth is that we were both quite similar in our leadership styles and personality types.

Over the time we worked together, I would constantly challenge her thinking and ask her to change things. Often, I did it to spite her (yes, I know how childish that sounds now). But I didn't know much better at the time.

That was until I read *Personality Plus* by Florence Littauer. Then I realised I was a 'Powerful Choleric', according to her definition. So was my marketing manager. The more I learned about the different personality types, the more it helped me to connect with others.

A few months after reading the book, I commented to my wife that I was really pleased with the progress my marketing manager had made and how I observed profound changes in her behaviour. Kay looked at me and, with a smile on her lips, announced, "She hasn't changed one bit, Elias. It's you who's changing!"

I had no idea that by changing myself and my behaviour, I could positively affect another person's perception.

After I left that role, I continued to invest in myself. I was insatiable in my pursuit of personal development and the art of growing me. Quite by chance, about eight years after we parted company, I happened to see that marketing manager in the building I was working in. We shared a brief conversation about her progress since we parted. And as we caught the lift to go our separate ways, I simply reached out to her and begged her forgiveness for the way I had treated her all those years earlier. At last, I experienced closure on that chapter of my life.

Are You Willing to Share Your Vulnerability?

We all make decisions that, with hindsight, we regret. The question is: How do you address the consequences of those mistakes? My first full-time job transported me abruptly into my leadership journey. Within six weeks of joining the company, I had been promoted to head the Electronic Production Team.

With that honour came a responsibility. I was only twenty-two years old, yet I was leading the largest department, with twenty-three people reporting to me. I was wet behind the ears and very green to the concept of leadership.

One day, I was approached by one of our high voltage assembly technicians. He was concerned that the members of the mechanical production team were receiving 50 pence per hour more than he was. I thanked him for bringing this to my attention, but I quickly dismissed the conversation and continued with my work.

A few weeks later, I was ushered into the office of our Human Resources Manager. The employee had taken his concern to the HR department and complained about my lack of response to his enquiry. This, I found out, would be the equivalent of what we now refer to as a personal grievance.

I was astounded! After all, it was only 50 pence per hour. As I was already on an annualised salary, it did not register with me that this small increment could possibly have much impact on someone's take home pay.

The reality of the situation was that it meant the whole world to him, and I had disrespected him and his concern. Our HR Manager was a very understanding lady, and she helped me to see the error of my way.

When I returned to my office, I called the whole department to a meeting and asked them to close the doors to give us privacy. Gathered in front of me were men and women, aged from our sixteen-year-old apprentice to our sixty-four-year-old, soon-to-be retiree. I cleared my throat and proceeded to explain why I had gathered them.

I explained the issue and gave them the background story that led to my conversation with HR. I confessed that I had acted in-appropriately and wanted to acknowledge publicly my mistake and the distress I had caused. I went on to ask for forgiveness and made a commitment to providing them with a better level of support and leadership going forward.

After I had said my piece and taken a question or two from the floor, we closed the meeting and opened the doors to our department. I returned to my office and left the door open as was my tradition. Within moments, Brian, my senior charge hand, came in and closed the door behind him. That was un-usual since he never came to see me. It also felt ominous that he would close the door behind him. I had that sinking feeling enter my stomach, and I wanted to crawl into a hole and die.

"In all the time that I've worked," Brian opened the conversation, "I have never seen anybody come forward and apologise like you did. I take my hat off to you, mate! That was incredible."

His words floored me. All I thought I had been doing was 'fessing up to my mistake. Taking it on the chin. Yet it became a valuable leadership lesson for me that I have tried to maintain throughout my life.

What are you willing to do to take ownership of your actions? Are you able to take the time to confess your mistake and allow others to see you are vulnerable and real? Or will you always hide behind an iron curtain to keep your feelings safe?

Take the time to write down when you have observed other leaders sharing their vulnerability and what outcomes you observed.

LEADER	EXAMPLE OF VULNERABILITY	OUTCOME

Applying lessons from Nelson Mandela's life:

Key #6 - LEADING FROM THE FRONT

On May 10th, 1994, Mandela was inaugurated as the first black President of South Africa. But his ability to lead from the front started a lot earlier in his career.

In 1944, Mandela joined the African National Congress (ANC) and worked with fellow party members, including Oliver Tambo, to establish its youth league, the ANCYL. Following the 1948 election victory of the Afrikaner-dominated National Party, which introduced a formal system of racial classification and segregation, Mandela's commitment to politics and the ANC grew stronger.

The introduction of apartheid, a system that restricted non-whites' basic rights and barred them from government while maintaining white minority rule, fuelled Mandela's desire to combat this oppression. His leadership, amongst others in the ANCYL, required years of petitioning for the ANC to adopt its plan to achieve full citizenship for all South Africans through boycotts, strikes, civil disobedience, and other non-violent methods.

Mandela helped lead the ANC's 1952 Campaign for the Defiance of Unjust Laws, travelling across the country to organise protests against discriminatory policies, and promoted the manifesto known as the Freedom Charter. By default, Mandela was speaking to groups of volunteers and leading them from the front. This culminated in a rally with about ten thousand people in attendance. It was held in Durban on June 22nd, and Mandela became the main speaker.

Not trained in the art of speaking, Mandela had to take the leadership position in this area. Whether speaking to a mass of people, or to an audience of a few dozen, Mandela made sure he took the same care to ensure that the matters he wanted to talk about were discussed in detail. He would not compress his message, nor would he skirt away from the truth. That is one of the characteristics of a leader who leads from the front....

"After climbing a great hill, one only finds that there are many more hills to climb."

— Nelson Mandela

Key #7

SURROUNDING YOURSELF WITH PEOPLE YOU CAN TRUST

"Integrity is doing the right thing,
even when no one is watching."

— C.S. Lewis

Treating people with respect and owning up to your mistakes are some of the leadership lessons that Key #6 dealt with. But as a leader, you need to have a team that surrounds you in order to lead with influence. This next key allows you to look at your team members and how they can affect your leadership results.

Whom Do You Turn to When You Have to Make the Big Decisions?

A few years ago, I made the big move and gave up my corporate job with all its bells and whistles.

Starting up my own business seemed like the logical thing to do, but it proved to be one of the hardest. With no defined income, no clients waiting in the wings, and no products to sell, I created a challenge for myself!

During the start-up phase, I came across an opportunity to launch something called 'Leadercast'. It was a whole day leadership training program, featuring a number of presenters, including Jim Collins (author of *Good to Great* and *How the Mighty Fall*) and my personal mentor and leadership guru, Dr John C. Maxwell.

The presenters were certainly top draw cards and respected in their individual fields. The challenge was that the Leadercast format was not well-known in New Zealand. The potential cost for me to promote the event was $30,000—and I only had three weeks to make a go/no-go decision as to whether I invested the money (which I didn't have) and risk my marriage if it failed.

In his book *The 21 Irrefutable Laws of Leadership*, John Maxwell identifies The Law of the Inner Circle. Maxwell goes on to say, "Nobody does anything great alone. Leaders do not succeed alone. A leader's potential is determined by those closest to him. What makes the difference is the leader's inner circle."

What I believe Maxwell is saying here directly applies to us as leaders within our own businesses. Whom do we go to for guidance on the topics that require an external and objective perspective?

In my case, I needed to make sure I didn't make a critical decision in isolation. I ended up identifying five key people whom I approached to become my personal board of directors. The people I chose were identified based on two key criteria:

1. Their business acumen
2. Their spiritual oversight

I chose to meet up with them individually over coffee and ran the ideas past them. Then I invited them to join me in a group meeting where I laid out the opportunity I had.

And the result of that meeting...? I ended up with nineteen critical questions to ask the organiser that I had not considered previously! By the time I received the answers, I reported back to my inner circle, and the advice given to me by all five was not to proceed with the Leadercast program at that point in time.

I believe that exercise helped me to save my business *and* my marriage.

Are You Strong Enough to Take the Truth If It Is Punched at You?

At times, you will need to seek counsel from those who surround you. It isn't always an easy thing to go up to somebody and ask for help.

During my business' infancy, my wife and I were experiencing issues. It's not that we had a bad marriage; it was just that the stress of our financial situation was starting to take a toll on our relationship.

Once my wife and I decided that we needed help, we applied a similar process to the inner circle to our situation. We opted to spend some time with two of the elders in our church.

First, I attended a meeting with the elders but not with my wife. The three of us met in a small room. I was asked to share my perspective on where I saw my business heading and how I felt it was affecting my marriage. I believe I was open about the truth of my situation and felt I had handled the questions accurately and honestly.

What I hadn't anticipated was the strong backlash I would encounter from the elders sitting opposite me. I was questioned about my decision-making process and whether I was on the right track. As the barrage of questions were fired my way, I truly felt as if I had gone through ten rounds with Mike Tyson!

I was reeling as I left the room. But I continued to search deep within me to ensure that I was honest and objective with my review. As a man of faith, I had to ask myself whether I was really hearing the voice of God directing my path or whether I needed to quit my business and stack shelves in my local supermarket to make money so we could pay our bills. My soul-searching provided me with the clarity I needed, and I continued along the same pathway I had started down.

Getting an independent review of your business can be dangerous, unless you have the fortitude to dig deep for the right answers. Are you willing to trust others to ask you the tough questions? Will you buckle under the stress of the questions that come your way? More importantly, are you willing to subject yourself to this form of independent review to get you on the right pathway for your business? A strong leader will listen to advice that he might not like to hear, but he will have the wisdom to remove his ego from the frame to accomplish the task ahead.

Is There Someone Willing to Mentor You?

Seeking counsel from somebody is the sign of a good leader. Having a person appear in your life and offer to mentor you is a stroke of luck that you should latch on to with both hands.

During the mid-1990s, when I was working in the UK, I held the role of marketing manager for Olivetti. At the time, we were developing a product in conjunction with British Telecom (BT). It involved a desktop PC, a phone, a video camera, and a computer unit, all connected to an ISDN line. (That's the original version of the digital phones we now know and love!) It allowed people to host videoconferencing calls, to share remote documents, and to annotate documents that were shared on a virtual whiteboard with other users anywhere around the world. We called it the P.C.C.—Personal Communications Computer.

Today, they call it Skype.

At the time, I was in my mid-twenties, and I still had a lot to learn. But due to the nature of our product and the marketing machine that ran behind both organisations, we ended up having the P.C.C. featured in a number of British newspapers.

I could have easily let the glamour of seeing my picture in the press and reading quotes attributed to me go to my head. Fortunately, I had a seasoned senior executive from our headquarters in Italy take me under his wing.

He was willing to mentor me and show me the ropes. Whenever he was in the UK, he would put aside time to catch up with me and to ask me questions about my role. We would regularly connect and invest time—usually over a coffee—once every two months. He also made sure that if I were visiting our offices in Italy, he would put aside an afternoon to take me through my paces.

This level of investment was something I originally took for granted. It was only with hindsight that I recognised the investment he made in me and the privilege of receiving his gift.

I now try to make sure I am mentoring two or three people at any one time.

Take a few minutes to think through people who have been influencers in your life. Describe the areas where they took you under their wing and mentored you. Identify the impact it had on your life.

NAME OF MENTOR	IMPACT ON MY LIFE

Are You Choosing Your Friends Carefully?

I once heard Charlie 'Tremendous' Jones speak at a live event in Auckland, New Zealand. He was in his eighties and nearing the end of his life. But that didn't diminish from his presentation, which he closed off in his signature style with the comment, "The person you are in five years is determined by the people you know and the books you read!" Around the same time, I heard Jim Rohn say, "You are the average of the five people you spend your time with."

Who are you spending your time with?

I am a driven individual, and I've always been a high achiever. Well, at least I've always desired to be a high achiever. Since these two thoughts kept crossing my mind, I started to ponder them.

As I looked at my bank balance one day, it dawned on me that my net worth *is* the average of the five people I spend most of my time with. So I made a conscious decision to evaluate whom I spent my time with.

In the Law of the Inner Circle, Maxwell describes people as carrying two buckets in their hands—one full of water and the second full of gasoline. How we choose to use each bucket can determine whether we are adding value to others or subtracting it from them.

Are You an Igniter or an Extinguisher?

When I lived in the UK, my ex-wife would share great ideas, like opening a daycare centre in our house. So I enthusiastically encouraged her by highlighting the steps behind this venture: gaining the council approvals, researching the market, and developing a full business plan for the bank. Her task list grew as I spoke. Whilst I must admit that I enjoyed the ensuing silence, it took me about two days to realise she wasn't talking to me because she was upset!

How do you know whether the people you are associating with are adding value to you or subtracting it from you? Here are five simple questions to ask yourself about the people who surround you:

1. **Do they lift you up or push you down?** It takes more effort to push somebody down than it does to lift him up. If you feel uplifted when you meet with somebody, make sure that you nurture that relationship. If the person pulls you down, it may be time for you to start walking away.
2. **Do they deposit into you or withdraw from you?** Are you enriched from an interaction with somebody, where she adds value to your thinking? Or does she leave you feeling drained, having subtracted some of your energy? I would encourage you to evaluate your 'bank balance' with people and determine when it's appropriate to close an overdrawn account.
3. **Do you look forward to meeting them or cringe when you spot them?** There are people who automatically bring a smile to my face. I look forward to talking to them and gaining from their wisdom. But similarly, there are others who make me shake my head at the thought of crossing paths with them. If they make you cringe, straighten your back, politely tell them that you can't stay long talking, and quietly walk away. And put some safe distance between them and you!
4. **Do they expand your thinking, or is it the 'same old, same old' with them?** A wise proverb states, "One bad apple spoils the barrel." If someone is rotting, remove him or her from your barrel of friends so you can save the fruit of your hard work.
5. **Do you aspire to be like them, or are you setting the pace?** If you aspire to reach a new level through someone's in-

> spirational leadership, then you should hold on to that relationship. But if you set the pace in the relationship, chances are that you're in the driver's seat. Look for someone who can do the driving, whilst you become the passenger, and learn from him or her during this journey.

So, the next time you interact with others, ask yourself these five questions to help you liberate your leadership potential!

How Much Can You Trust Others?

If the last story showed the damaging effect of pouring water over somebody's dream, this one will show the dangers of pouring gasoline on a flammable situation. When I was about four or five years old, I am told, I approached my mum and asked her for a knife, so I could stab my father in the back and kill him!

Now, I can't tell you whether this was a true event or a planted memory. All I know is that over the years, my mum would repeat this story to me and anybody else who was willing to listen. Combine this with my father calling me an idiot, and I would like to pose the following question, "How do you think that affected my relationship with my father?"

Needless to say, we had a strained and somewhat dysfunctional relationship whilst I was growing up. My viewpoint of my father was somewhat coloured by my mum's comments.

As a leader, we are all affected by external sources. Our worldview is tainted by what others do and say about us and the people we interact with. Who is currently influencing your thinking?

Can you trust those who surround you? As previously mentioned, Charlie 'Tremendous' Jones challenges us to think about the people we meet and the books we read.

If you want your thinking to change, ask yourself, "Who am I spending most of my time with?" At the same time, challenge yourself by analysing what you are reading that, in turn, you are using to feed your mind?

Are you being supplied with false information by a close friend or family member that is being used to poison your views on someone? Maybe you are not aware of what is going on insipidly in the background. If the person is constantly negative, chances are it is rubbing off on you.

I once challenged a team I was leading to go back and review the impact others were having on their lives. To my surprise, the following Monday morning at our tea break, one of my direct reports came bounding into the kitchen with a massive smile beaming across her face.

She went on to tell me that after our conversation, she was at home with her mother and sister watching TV over the weekend. For the first time, she took notice of the tone and content of their comments and realised how negative they were being. She stood up and told them she felt they were negative and rude about others. But she didn't stop there. She politely asked them to leave her house and gave them instructions that they were only welcome back once they returned with positive attitudes!

Now that's what I call radical. When I asked her how she felt about it, she told me it was one of the most cleansing experiences she'd had—ever!

So before you go out and shoot the messenger, take some time to consider the impact of your decision to cut off certain relationships within your sphere of influence. You might start off by telling people something similar to this: "Thanks for your comments, Steven, but I think that what you are saying borders on gossip. I'd like to steer away from that going forward if you don't mind."

This could become your gateway to an alternative path that separates you from others' negativity. At the end of the day, you need to ensure that you can surround yourself with people you can trust.

Applying lessons from Nelson Mandela's life:

Key #7 - SURROUNDING YOURSELF WITH PEOPLE YOU CAN TRUST

Whilst in Robben Island, the ANC formed its own internal organisation, known as the High Command or, more officially, the High Organ. Most of the senior members of the ANC who had served on the National Executive also served on the High Organ.

Walter Sisulu, Govan Mbeki, and Raymond Mhlaba were founding members of the High Organ. Their names, amongst others like Oliver Tambo, Moses Kotane, Ahmed Kathrada, and Joe Slovo, appear many times throughout Mandela's book *Long Walk to Freedom.*

Mandela first met Sisulu in 1941. Tambo made his acquaintance in 1943. Kathrada, Slovo, and Kotane met Mandela a few years later in the late 1940s. In the 1950s, he met Mbeki, Mhlaba, and others who became close acquaintances and influencers. Yet all of these people, whether they were local to Mandela or in distant lands, provided him with his inner circle of trusted advisors. Even when Mandela became isolated from his inner circle as he was imprisoned in Pollsmoor Prison, he still maintained direct communication with them whenever practical to ensure he could keep to the path that the ANC chose to travel....

"Whatever position I occupied, it was the result of colleagues—of my comrades in the movement—who had decided in their wisdom to use me for the purpose of focusing the attention of the country and the international community on me."

— Nelson Mandela

Key #8

DOING THE RIGHT THING

"I follow three rules: Do the right thing, do the best you can, and always show people you care."

— Lou Holtz

Now that we have discussed the key on surrounding yourself with people you can trust, let us explore the way we interact with others. In this key, we will look at the ethical side of leadership and how people behave. Recently, we have seen a blurring of the line between what was once viewed as right and wrong. The examples I will use in this key are not a judgement call on the individuals mentioned, but more of a tapestry for you to use as a backdrop to your own value system.

Are You Doing the Right Thing?

For those who do not know Lou Holtz, he is a legend in American college football coaching and the only coach in NCAA history to lead six different programs to bowl games. He is best known for his role in coaching Notre Dame—the Fighting

Irish—to multiple successes, and he is also a multiple winner of National Coach of the Year honours.

As a coach, Holtz was successful beyond measure, and he knew how to get the best out of his players. After all, it has been said that coaching is about influencing the lives of young people.

When it came to leadership, Holtz said, "I can name you the coach, but I cannot name you the leader. Leaders are named from below."

Holtz made the following assumptions of all his college athletes:

- They wanted to graduate.
- They wanted to be champions.
- They wanted to perform at their best.
- They wanted to help the team.
- They wanted to make positive contributions.

Over the years, the slender, bespectacled Holtz lived by three rules:

1. Do the right thing!
2. Do your best.
3. Treat people well.

These three rules translated into three essential questions, which he encouraged each member of his playing team to ask each other:

- Do you trust me (on and off the field)?
- Are you committed? (There are to be no pretenders or imposters).

- Do you care about me?

These questions needed to be answered if the team members were to build strong relationships with each other.

Trust is built on the back of doing the right things. This concept was brought to my attention through a client. As mentioned in Key #3, I worked for a company that outsourced the contact centres for our local telecommunications company. We employed a staff of about 400, and we were responsible for answering directory assistance calls (when someone called up to find out the phone number for an individual or a business) as well as handling the front-line calls on behalf of the emergency services (police, fire, or ambulance).

During our annual retreat with our client, when we went through the goals and objectives for the forthcoming year, our client stepped up to the front of the room and started to deliver his vision. He spoke about the financial goals he wanted us to achieve. Details were shared on the improvement in the metrics for our call answering times, abandon rates, and average call length. These were lofty goals that would stretch us all.

Then he concluded his presentation with the following statement. "I want you to do the right thing—don't do things right!"

It took me a while to grasp what he was instructing us to do.

Process is an important component of every successful organisation. We have processes established to ensure that things get done and items don't fall between the cracks. The clearer the definitions of each process, the more likely you will get a successful outcome.

What our client was advocating was that we should not sacrifice the customer experience for the desire to follow the process to the letter. His instructions got me thinking....

If you've had the opportunity to work in a call centre, you know that they are usually driven by the metrics. The team leaders monitor the number of incoming calls, the abandon rates, the average length of each call, and even the timing and length of breaks! Everything seems to be micromanaged.

'Doing the right thing' is a key principle that puts the concept of 'following the rules' on its head. Whilst not advocating a revolution, this principle encourages us to think about the outcome for our client and to ensure that the process is secondary to it. It challenges us to understand the motivation of both parties and to determine whether the chosen pathway would deliver the right outcome.

Another way to look at it is by asking the question, "Are you looking for pleasing methods (process), or pleasing results (outcomes)?" Personally, I'm always looking for pleasing results.

As a leader, are you doing the right thing? Are you able to look beyond the 'way we do things' to ensure that you look after your people and put them first? Whether it's an internal member of staff, a supplier, or a customer, you can build trust by doing the right thing.

Take the time to fill in the box below and think of pleasing methods vs. pleasing results that you are looking for in your organisation:

PLEASING METHOD	PLEASING RESULT

What Would You Do If Your Business Colleague Started to Shoplift in Front of You?

When I was working in the UK, I remember taking a roadtrip with one of the salesmen in our company. We were visiting new prospects with the objective of bringing them on as clients. I was there to help answer operational and logistical questions that my team would be addressing when the account was landed.

It was the first time I'd had an opportunity to work with this colleague. He had been with us for less than six months, so I had only observed him at a distance.

When we were returning home, we stopped in one of the service stations that dotted the UK landscape alongside the motorway system. Having stretched our legs and taken a toilet break, we went to the petrol station and refuelled.

As I approached the pay station, I noticed that my colleague picked up some confectionery, which he proceeded to place into his pocket. I must admit that I did a double-take. Needless to say, he walked out without paying for his sweet-tooth's obsession.

I confronted him as we returned to the car. When I told him I had observed what he had done, I asked him whether he had any intention of paying for it. His response was very matter-of-fact.... The company running the service station was already making a large profit—it was the company's expectation that a proportion of its stock would be stolen.

His answer sent shivers down my spine. Whatever credibility he might have had with me prior to this incident vapourised instantly. I did an about turn, returned to the cashier, explained that my colleague had inadvertently walked away without paying for his purchases, and settled his account. Needless to say, I never worked with him again.

What do you think the right thing to do would have been in this instance? Would you have 'taken what was yours' on the back of the 'greedy profits' made by a multinational? Would you have been able to sleep at night with a clear conscience? Or would you have taken him to task and called him out to both the retailer and his boss?

This is the challenge of 'doing the right thing'.

How Would You Respond to Allegations that Your Products Led to the Deaths of Seven People?

In the fall of 1982, McNeil Consumer Products, a subsidiary of Johnson & Johnson, was confronted with a crisis when seven people on Chicago's West Side died mysteriously. Investigations by the authorities determined that each of the deceased had ingested an Extra-Strength Tylenol capsule laced with cyanide. This news travelled quickly and was the cause of a massive, nationwide panic.

The challenge for the parent company, Johnson & Johnson, was that immediate action was required to arrest the decline of consumer confidence and show the company's strength and leadership to an already spooked consumer base. Its course of action was to launch an instant public relations program, including the immediate voluntary removal and destruction of $100 million of stock from the shelves.

This brave move showed the integrity of the company and its leadership. Few would have been brave enough to step up and do the right thing.

Are You Willing to Take Responsibility for Your Own Actions?

A few years ago, I did something so dumb that it almost cost me my career. Whilst enjoying a coffee with some colleagues, my cellphone rang. Although I didn't recognise the number, I took the call nonetheless.

"Good morning. This is Elias," I answered.

"Elias, this is the company's legal counsel calling. We haven't met before, but I need to talk to you about something quite urgent." From the caller's tone, I realised this was a serious call and required immediate and private attention.

"Sure thing," I replied. "Let me just get to a place where I have a little privacy."

I got up from the table and walked outside the cafe where I was out of earshot from my colleagues.

My heartbeat started to race as the caller asked me about an affidavit I had recently submitted in relation to a patents claim. Immediately, my heart sank to the pit of my stomach and I knew something was adrift.

A few months prior to the call, I had been approached by a colleague with a request for assistance. It transpired that he had a close friend in Wellington who was a patent attorney. The attorney was looking for somebody who was an expert in the area of call centres and needed to gain some context for the use of technology at the turn of the millennium.

In particular, the attorney was trying to determine whether texting was a common method of communicating with customer service representatives (CSRs) in contact centres back in 2001.

It was my opinion that texting was not a common practice within the industry, and I referred back to a role I had with another organisation I was working for at the time to reference my experience. Whilst I was offered some form of remuneration for the time I took to get my affidavit drafted and certified, I declined the offer of any payment and was happy to offer the service pro bono to help my colleague out.

The trouble, it turned out, was that the attorney who collected my affidavit was working on behalf of an organisation that was using it to sue one of my company's major customers. And my expert opinion could have the undesired impact of a multi-million dollar lawsuit!

I knew my only option was to confess to my involvement and seek immediate resolution with the legal counsel.

"I'm at fault here," I stated. "I now realise that what I did was wrong, and as an employee of the company, I should have sought legal advice before offering my experience. I think the right thing to do is to offer you my resignation and, if you agree, then I'm willing to offer it here and now."

As I spoke, I felt that sickening sensation that had plagued me many times in my career as I found myself teetering on the brink of self-destruction once again.

The legal counsel paused and told me she would think about my offer and get back to me.

I confirmed to her that my next step would be to contact the patent attorney and withdraw my expert testimony, which I did straight after the call was completed.

I then phoned my immediate boss to explain the blunder I had made and its implication. Once again, I offered my resignation and asked her for some advice.

"Hang tight, Elias," she replied. "Let me see what I can find out."

After an anxious forty-eight hours waiting to hear back, I received a second call from the legal counsel.

"We've reviewed the situation, Elias, and we have decided not to accept your resignation." The words drew a huge sigh of relief from me. "We believe you operated in innocence—albeit rather naively—and your remorse was genuine. We'll just chalk this up to experience and leave it at that."

If you've made the mother of all blunders at work, how would you address it? Are you willing to put your hand up and accept full responsibility? Even if the consequences are that you could lose your job?

As I look back at this situation, I have to confess that I would not do anything differently. I needed to take the medicine that was dished out in this situation and ensure that I was accountable for my actions. To coin a popular phrase, "You do the crime, you do the time!"

Is It Possible to Be Objective?

As I've already alluded to earlier in this book, I'm an avid football fan. I enjoy the game, but more recently, I've hung up my playing boots and watched from the sidelines. That was until I was persuaded to sit for my referee's ticket!

To be honest, there's little gratitude shown towards referees. The fans think you are blind and deaf. Sometimes, I wish I was!

As a referee, you have to have a strong grip on the game because you often have to make instantaneous decisions that can turn a match. There is little room for error. As if I didn't think the pressure to perform was great enough, I was tested when I was asked to referee my son's school games.

When it comes to taking the field, a referee must be impartial and put aside personal relationships. If you consider that in New Zealand, as I found out when I first arrived, you can become best of friends within five minutes and find out that you are related to each other within ten, then being impartial takes a lot of discipline.

The same concept applies with leadership. As a leader, you often need to be conscious of the relationships and history between yourself and others you are dealing with. But you also need to push aside any feelings that could colour your judgement.

It is often said that leaders get paid the big bucks to address the big hitting issues within an organisation. Whether it is related to a financial outcome, or the redeployment of individuals during a right-sizing campaign, as a leader, you need to ensure that you are always seen as walking on the side of integrity.

Here's a three-point process you can use to help you stay impartial:

1. **Disclose your interests.** If you have a relationship with an individual or an organisation that could provide a conflict of interest down the track, make sure people are aware of it before you start your negotiations.
2. **Use the 'kitchen noticeboard test'.** Ask yourself the following question, "How would I feel if people were to see [this] posted on the noticeboard in the kitchen for public consumption?" If it can cause embarrassment, then refrain from doing it.
3. **Avoid getting drawn into the emotion of the situation.** As a referee, you will often get the shout from both the players and the supporters when they want to influence your decisions. As a leader, you need to be in control of your emotions and not allow yourself to be sucked in and

sidetracked by others. Whilst this might sound difficult to achieve in the short term, it can be mastered through positive reinforcement.

What Have You Been Carrying?

Being impartial means you have no leaning one way or another. An impartial person does not hang on to specific viewpoints that can influence his or her decisions.

There's a great story about two monks who are walking beside the river when they come across a beautiful young woman wearing a spectacular new outfit. It becomes instantly apparent to the monks that she is facing a dilemma...she needs to cross the river, but she doesn't want to dirty her new dress.

The first monk asks her whether she needs assistance to cross the river, to which she replies in the affirmative.

He instructs her to jump on his back and proceeds to carry her across the river, depositing her safely on the other side. The monks then bid farewell to her and they and she continue their journeys in opposite directions.

After an hour, the second monk turns around to the first monk and admonishes him.

"You know, my brother," the second monk says, "we're not allowed to speak to or touch women in our monastery. And you did both!"

"I know, my friend," the first monk replies. "But here's the interesting point. I put her down an hour ago, yet you are still holding on to her!"

How often do people tend to hold on to things from the past, unable (or unwilling) to let them go. These habits can sometimes become the crutches that turn us into bitter and subjective individuals. We allow these experiences to cloud our judgement as leaders.

To enable you to do the right thing, make sure you let go of the past and focus on the future. That is why God created you with your head facing forward. Otherwise, if He had wanted you to focus on the past, He would have placed your head facing backwards!

Applying lessons from Nelson Mandela's life:

Key #8 - DOING THE RIGHT THING

U.S. President Bill Clinton, in the introduction he wrote to the 2013 edition for Mandela's book, *Long Walk to Freedom*, introduces his observations on Mandela. I am drawn to this text because it challenges our thinking about the damage that prison could have caused to Mandela.

During one conversation, Clinton questions Mandela's ability to forgive his captors and asks whether he would hate them all over again. Mandela had the maturity in his leadership to let it all go. It was something that he needed to do to keep his mind and his heart because he knew he would need both to lead his country. "To make peace with an enemy one must work with your enemy, and that enemy becomes one's partner," Mandela concluded.

What will it take for you to forgive your enemies? And what has to change in your heart to enable you to do the right thing, even though every fibre in your body would scream at you to travel in the opposite direction...?

"We must use time wisely and forever realize that the time is always ripe to do right."

— Nelson Mandela

Key #9

RECRUITING PEOPLE WITH A GOOD ATTITUDE

"It isn't what you have or who you are or where you are or what you are doing that makes you happy or unhappy. It is what you think about it."

— Dale Carnegie

If doing the right thing is a prerequisite in a leader's arsenal, the next key for a good leader is to recruit people with a good attitude. What good is there in doing the right thing and having a good attitude yourself, if that is not reflected in those who surround you? Whilst skills to do a role are important, attitude is critical. You can train people and up-skill them to help deliver a role, but it becomes increasingly difficult to change a person's attitude. In fact, that can take a lifetime to accomplish!

Who Is Joining Your Team?

In the late 1990s, I was approached by my accountant, Clive, and his wife, Helen. After months of constant reminders from Clive that I must diversify, I was persuaded to allow them to present the Amway business plan to me and my wife Kay.

I was aware that they were going to talk to me about the Amway business because the hallway leading to Clive's office was lined with shelves full of SA8 Laundry Powder and bottles of L.O.C. For a long time, I had resisted their approaches. Resigned to hearing them share this opportunity with me, I was convinced that I would be able to tick off that box and carry on with my life.

No one was more surprised than me to hear the simplicity of the plan and the benefits I would enjoy by joining up as an independent business owner. I did, however, promise Kay that we would not make a decision about the business during Clive and Helen's visit, and I kept that promise. The following day, we were invited to attend a business development seminar, which introduced us to a wider group of positive people. This was one of the few times I could remember being surrounded by people with a good attitude.

It was infectious! I wanted some of that for myself. Think about the people on your team. Do they have a good attitude? Or are you dealing with a 'Charlie'?

You may have heard the classic golfing joke where a man returns home to tell his wife about the dramatic events that unfurled earlier that day on the golf course.

"It was a bad day at the course," he tells his wife. "Charlie had a heart attack on the third hole."

"That's terrible!" she says.

"You're telling me. All day long, it was hit the ball, drag Charlie."

How draining would it be to have to drag 'Charlie' and his bad attitude behind you all day long? Would you prefer to replace him with people who have a good attitude? As a strong leader, you have to have those courageous conversations that let the

'Charlies' in your life know that they either have to improve their characters or you will have to release them from your life. Don't spend the rest of your life 'hitting the ball and dragging Charlie'!

Are You Being True to Your Convictions?

Paul Martinelli, the President of the John Maxwell Team (JMT), is famous for encouraging his clients to "Hold Your Image!" I've had the privilege of being mentored by him since I joined the JMT in 2011.

Having a leader with immense capacity has been a godsend to me as I started my fledging business. More than once, I have wanted to quit, but then I would hear Paul's words echo in my ears: "Elias, do you have the courage to continue? Because more things are possible!"

Recently, a good friend of mine had a real dilemma she had to address. She had a burning desire to share a message with a group from the local area where she had grown up. However, as time drew nearer to the day of her conference, she hit a crisis point with less than a third of the necessary seats sold for her to break even.

And the doubt crept in....

She had to make a critical decision either to pull the plug, let some people down, and lose some money on the venture...or carry on with the risk that nobody else would register to attend and she would lose even more money!

Thankfully, she sought help!

You've probably heard the proverb, "Where there is no counsel, the people fall." My friend had the presence of mind to seek advice from her inner circle group. I say that because another old proverb says, "In the multitude of counsellors, there is safety."

When she realised that making that decision in isolation was a risk, she acknowledged that she was in a space where her reasoning might be impaired by her emotions and her lack of energy. The group she approached for advice challenged her thinking and asked her to review her motivation for the conference. After much soul-searching, she concluded that the event would go on and she would stick to her guns! I'm pleased to announce that her hard work paid off since her event was well-attended and delivered a profit.

So the next time you find yourself up against the odds with a project you have started but that you are unsure you should complete, here are five simple things that may help you stay on track, maximise your potential, and lift yourself to the next level:

1. **Stick to your guns:** Ask yourself, "Why did I embark on this project in the first place?" If your motivation was initially flawed, your project is doomed to failure. However, we sometimes get distracted along the path of life and end up off course. Stop what you are doing, review the background behind your decision, rediscover the passion that originally stoked the fire, and use that motivation to start rekindling the flame.
2. **Stick to your position:** When you know beyond any doubt that you are on the right path, stick to your position! Do not deviate from the path ahead, no matter how steep it is. As a cycling friend of mine once said, "At the end of every steep hill is a downhill leg!" Push through that uphill path and enjoy a less tiring downhill glide!
3. **Stick to your beliefs:** My son invented his own board game at holiday camp. In his game, he had 'Chances' and 'Problems'. If you landed on a 'Chance', you would be blessed with a move to the next 'Chance', a move forward of twenty-five spaces or even 'Go to the end &

win!' However, his 'Problem' cards could have you going back seventeen spaces or—worse still—missing seven turns! If you believe that your rewards are huge and your penalties severe, I would encourage you to stick to your beliefs and the truth they represent to you rather than being sidetracked by popular folklore.

4. **Stick to your faith:** If you are a person of faith, set aside some time to ask the Grand Overall Designer (G.O.D.) for some guidance. As John Maxwell describes in one of his Minute with Maxwell videos, having effective faith is having a combination of believing in the G.O.D., yourself, and other people. Be willing to bet on yourself, use the strength of the G.O.D., and believe that people can make a difference in other people's lives.

5. **Stick to your convictions:** When you have a hard row to hoe, draw deeply from your inner strength and resolve to succeed. Look for the support to get you through those tough times. As I've said a number of times in the past, even the best leaders can't do it on their own. They need a team around them that completes them, not one that competes against them! Make sure the foundations of your conviction are deeply rooted; then you will be able to withstand the toughest storms that blow through!

So the next time you find yourself facing a tough decision, remember to stick to your convictions and use these five tips to get you to the other side!

What Will Make You Fall from Grace?

At one point, Lance Armstrong was the darling of the cycling world. He had overcome adversity, including surviving testicular cancer, to become a legend. The winner of seven consecutive Tour de France races from 1999-2005, Armstrong couldn't seem to do anything wrong.

Accusations, however, that he was taking performance enhancing drugs mounted over the years. He vehemently denied any wrongdoing. Blood and urine samples were tested and re-tested in an attempt to catch him out and validate the claims. But year after year, they came back negative, and these results upheld his position as the 'clean man' of the cycling world. Even a positive test for a banned substance during his first Tour de France win in 1999 was explained away by a prescription for a cream to treat saddle sores, but the doubts and rumours surrounding Armstrong refused to go away.

With sponsors backing him in ever-increasing circles, his actions elevated him to a position of cult status. Despite the gruelling format of the tour and the physical demands on his body due to horrific accidents that exposed bone, Armstrong always pulled through. He made headlines by shattering the world record number of wins for a single competitor.

But in 2012, his life was to shatter as he made the headlines again—this time for all the wrong reasons. It wasn't until 2013, eight years after his final Tour de France victory, that Armstrong admitted doping in an interview with Oprah Winfrey.

Armstrong lived and operated in a world where illicit drug taking amongst his peers was commonplace. Yet it was with a conscious decision that he continued that practice. Improvements in the techniques used for drug detection resulted in the outing of his drug-taking habits. Once a hero, Armstrong was stripped of his titles and accolades.

As a leader, you are responsible for your actions. When you start a lie, you have to continue living the lie. It always amuses me to see the lengths to which certain individuals or organisations will go to keep a lie alive. I would think it would take more effort to continue along that path than it would to come clean in the first place.

You may have heard the phrase, "You're either green and growing or ripe and rotting." Whatever goes into you will eventually have to come out of you. In Armstrong's case, it was the drugs that finally came out of his system that outed his behaviour. There would be no defence that could protect him.

How Loyal Are You?

Back in Key #1, I mentioned that I started a love-hate relationship with the Arsenal Football Club in 1971. Over that time, I have seen it win six domestic Championships, nine F.A. Cup competitions, the European Cup Winner Cup, seven F.A. Community Shields, and become the only team in the modern era that has completed a whole season undefeated (the infamous 'invincibles' of the 2003-2004 season).

The heady days of that season and those accomplishments have been followed by a barren spell of twelve seasons without a domestic championship win.

Loyalty is an important attribute of a strong leader. I believe it is a character trait that shines alongside trust and integrity. Therefore, my son has only seen me support one team. With the wealth of European teams that have dominated the football stage, including Barcelona, Real Madrid, Bayern Munich, AC Milan, and Manchester United, it is not uncommon for the younger fans to include other teams' shirts in their closets.

For me a more disturbing phenomenon is the emergence of teams like Manchester City and PSG (Paris Saint-Germain) where the wealth of a foreign investor has created 'super teams'. These investors have attracted the best talent from across the world and retained players who could create a meteoric rise in fortunes for their clubs.

These teams' performances have turned the heads of younger fans and the aspect of loyalty seems to be thrown aside, like a crushed Coke can! I see my son's friends arrive at our house to watch the live broadcast of an English Premier League match. wearing the shirts of their latest favourite teams.

Boys who once wore the red of Manchester United have swapped them for the sky-blue of its fierce cross-town rival, Manchester City. It would appear that these younger fans' loyalty is swayed as easily as wheat fields when the wind breathes over them.

If I were to allow my attitude to take over, I would have long ago shifted my loyalty from Arsenal to other teams. But I am pleased that I was able to make one decision, forty-five years ago, that I am able to adhere to.

As a leader, you need to have loyalty from, and express loyalty to, your people. They need to know you are willing to support them and 'take a bullet' for them, as you would hope that they would do for you. I have invested time with my most loyal followers to help develop them and learn more about them and what makes them tick. Unfortunately, I have made mistakes along the way, and I may even have thrown them 'under the bus'. On the few occasions that has happened, my first response was to admit my guilt, confess my sin, and make public my reparation of that situation. Keeping a good attitude has helped me to restore the relationship and maintain the momentum.

Take a few minutes to take stock of the key relationships you have. Write down on the list below the names of the most loyal people you have following you. Beside each name, document the last time you caught up with the person one-on-one. Identify how frequently you connect with each other (ideally in a face-to-face situation). Then determine whether the relationship is strong, in need of repair, or broken beyond repair. Identify those relationships that require attention, and create a plan to address that.

NAME	DATE OF LAST CONTACT	FREQUENCY OF MEETINGS	STRONG (S) REPAIR (R) BROKEN (B)

Are You Just A 'Little Old Kiwi from the North Shore'?

Shortly after I joined the JMT, I was selected to chair a couple of committees as we developed and launched the YouthMAX program. One of my responsibilities was to host calls that were attended by my peers from various geographies across the globe.

New Zealand, for those who have not visited our fair shore, is the furthest east that you can travel before crossing the date line. We have a reputation as a clean, green nation (100% Pure, as the New Zealand Marketing Board would lead you to believe). We are also the home to a flightless, nocturnal bird called the Kiwi, the national icon of New Zealand and our unofficial national emblem.

During the call, I would often say, "I'm just a little old Kiwi from the North Shore, here in Auckland!"

It was said to help others understand that they didn't have to be hot shots to participate in the program we were delivering. By making that declaration, I was in effect putting myself down. Yet it took me quite a while to realise the damage I was causing to myself. After a number of conversations with a variety of successful people within the JMT, I finally realised how my self-limiting beliefs were restricting my potential.

I used to think I was a positive person with a good and strong attitude. On the whole, most people would have agreed. But when you analysed it deeper, it became obvious that I was self-sabotaging!

I had to work hard to convince myself that I wasn't the idiot my father's word had led me to believe as I was growing up. I had to be honest with myself. As a man of faith, I was told that I was made in His image. If the G.O.D. was the maker of heaven and earth, of all things visible and invisible, who was I to make myself out to be just a 'little old Kiwi from the North Shore'?

I had to be honest with myself, and I had to work hard to retrain myself to believe I was meant to gain positions of responsibility and rewards commensurate with my capabilities.

Today, as I write this book, I find myself the National President of the National Speakers Association of New Zealand (NSANZ), a Member of the Executive Committee within the Global Speakers Federation (GSF), and commanding five-figure fees for keynotes and training programs I deliver worldwide.

As a leader, make sure you use this key when you recruit those who surround you. And remember to start with yourself as the first member of your team who is recruited.

Are You Standing for Something or Falling for Everything?

In 2007, I read the book *Eve's Bite* by investigative journalist, Ian Wishart. The dust jacket claims it is the most politically-incorrect book ever published, and it might be. It is a thoroughly researched and well-articulated insight into the origins of our current society's woes.

The book review on Amazon said:

> Imagine if one day, a la 'The Truman Show', you woke up to find that everything you believed was the result of a careful manipulation of your life by someone else? What if much of what you believed was a lie? Well, for you, that day has arrived. In an age dominated by 'Spin', you're about to discover that the best spin campaigns of all are the ones you never even knew about.
>
> In the most politically incorrect book ever published in this country, journalist Ian Wishart rounds up a herd of sacred cows, skewering the social engineers and exposing the elites who want your taxes and your children while they laugh all the way to the bank like perverse Pied Pipers.... *Eve's Bite*: Read it before they pass a law against it....

For too long, I was influenced by the media. Whether I wished to confess it or not, my beliefs had taken on a worldview. What I took as an absolute when I was younger had been manipulated by my surroundings.

As I read the book, it stirred a fire deep within my belly. I reflected on my behaviour and the impact it had on those who surrounded me. It made me reflect on what I had planned to do and compare it to what I was doing.

Are you happy with the status quo? Do you look back at your life and regret not doing something? Do you wish you could be a bigger catalyst and change agent?

Having this realisation was one of my defining moments. I wondered what I could do to take action. My own behaviour and thoughts had led me to the position I found myself in. There was nothing startling about where I found myself, but I knew that for me to make a change, I would have to become the change I wanted to see in the world!

My attitude was determining my outcome. I had to make a decision that would potentially change my family, my world, and my community. It was at that point that I made a decision to seek like-minded people and get involved in politics.

My journey took me to the formation of a Christian political party, called the Family Party, where I was originally a board member. With no political experience or aspirations, my self-belief soon grew as I became convicted by my belief system. I gained the courage to work alongside people like Richie Lewis and Paul Adams to understand more about what we might accomplish.

This journey led me to leaving my highly paid and comfortable role in the corporate world in exchange for volunteering to work for a year within the Family Party. Offered the role of Party President, I knew that by surrounding myself with positive, driven people, we could make this happen.

Was it easy? Not at all! Would I do it again? Yes—as long as two criteria were met: 1) that I was surrounded by a dozen strong and competent people, and 2) that we had $1 million backing us! I was living proof that having a good attitude can help you overcome not having the required skills for a role.

I want you to ask yourself, "What am I willing to fight for?" If you were to look back at your life from your deathbed, what regrets would you have? Take a few minutes to write down the things you would be willing to try if time and money were not a factor. And when you have completed this list, prioritise them from the most to least important. On the right-hand side of the list, document all the benefits the world would receive if you completed your list. Heck, what harm could this cause? It's only a dream after all.... And if you have a dream, remember that Dr Martin Luther King, Jr also 'had a dream'.

DREAM/ASPIRATION	PRIORITY

Applying lessons from Nelson Mandela's life:

Key #9 - RECRUITING PEOPLE WITH A GOOD ATTITUDE

During his stay in Robben Island, Mandela was subjected to a number of instances where he was charged with an offense that sent him into isolation. The wardens and commanding officers (CO) were often recruited from a group of people who were austere and able to toe the 'party line'. They were often hardnosed Afrikaners.

After they arrived at Robben Island, the prisoners had great difficulty getting their grievances heard. Whilst working in the lime quarry one day, the CO came to observe them with another gentleman, whom they soon recognised as Brigadier Aucamp.

Mandela put down his pick and began to walk over to them, knowing that he was violating regulations. He was hoping that it would offer him an opportunity to be heard in public. Unfortunately, it backfired since he ended up back in isolation. However, Mandela learnt a lesson from this experience. He realised that nobody, least of all a prison officer, likes to have his authority challenged in public.

Mandela noted in his book: "Aucamp would have to humiliate his subordinate. Prison officials responded much better to private overtures. The best way to effect change on Robben Island was to attempt to influence officials privately rather than in public."

Mandela knew it was important to maintain a good attitude at all times. Even the warders and COs were recruited because they had similar attitudes to each other. You could argue that they were negative individuals, racist and brutal, but collectively, they delivered the same format of justice.

The counterbalance that Mandela and the members of the High Organ gave was their determination that their own positive and good attitudes would sustain them through the brutal years they suffered under the hands of people like Aucamp.

Choose your attitude and choose it wisely; otherwise, your journey might be a long one in isolation....

"Prison was a kind of crucible that tested a man's character. Some men, under the pressure of incarceration, showed true mettle, while others revealed themselves as less than what they appeared to be."

— Nelson Mandela

Key #10

LEARNING IS YOUR RESPONSIBILITY

"Live as if you were to die tomorrow.
Learn as if you were to live forever."

— Mahatma Gandhi

Attitude, we have determined, is more important than skills in certain cases. This next key is based on the premise that learning is an ongoing process. And the responsibility for learning lies squarely at your feet. It is nobody else's. It starts in our youth and goes all the way to the grave. As you digest this key, I would encourage you to take a mental check on your current learning regime (if one actually exists) and measure your effectiveness against this key.

Are You a Super-Sub or Are You Committed to the Cause?

I love watching football. The legendary Pele coined the phrase "The beautiful game" to describe it.

When the Euro 2012 competition was coming to a close, a

number of late substitutions turned the games around. An underdog team had created an upset that surprised the world during the qualifying stages. But the teams left in the semi-finals all included one common thread...a strong youth development program!

The future of any organisation is often defined by the lifeblood of its next generation of leaders. And leaders, we all know, are not born—they develop over time.

Where do you sit on the scale of self-development? Are you willing to invest in yourself, or are you happy to be freed of the classroom's shackles?

Take the time to make an inventory of your self-development. Some will say that at the minimum, you should be investing 1 percent of your revenues in self-development. I would like to suggest 5 to 10 percent (and maybe even more when you first start off on your journey).

ITEMS I HAVE INVESTED IN	VALUE OF INVESTMENT

How Thick Can You Be and Still Breathe?

When I was growing up in the UK, my father told me I was an idiot, and my teachers reinforced this message a number of times. It was our school's practice in the 1970s to announce the individual results of each class, starting with the academic excellence of the top student and finishing on the head of the 'dunce' student at the bottom of the pile. Did you guess where I appeared in that list? [Here's a spoiler alert...if you don't want to find out, look away now and turn the page over!]

Yes, you guessed it. I was rock bottom! Year in, year out. I remember hearing a teacher sentencing me to a life of failure. "You'll end up in prison, Kanaris, the way you're going on!"

I was sentenced at age thirteen to a future as a failure. Unfortunately, my academic performance matched my teachers' expectations. I barely scraped through my exams, but I still managed to complete my Bachelor's Degree and a post-graduate Masters of Science.

Yet, despite these accomplishments, I still felt I was destined for mediocrity. I never expected to do much. My career provided supporting evidence to my beliefs. I rarely held on to a role for more than a year or two, and I was self-sabotaging at every opportunity.

In my attempt to reinvent myself, I left the UK and started a new life in New Zealand. But the patterns repeated themselves. I secured a job, and within a few years, I found myself on the unemployment scrapheap, searching for new roles.

The days turned into weeks, and the weeks turned into months. I eventually found myself walking down Queen Street and into the offices of a recruitment agency, which I had visited only twenty-four hours prior for some psychometric testing. I was ushered into a private room furnished with a simple table and two chairs. The comforting factor was that a window offered a lovely view across the water towards the North Shore and the Harbour Bridge.

"Well, the tests came in and I'm pleased to say that you are a really smart cookie! You scored in the top 0.1 percent on your IQ tests, and your profile matches that of a CEO," announced the recruitment consultant as he closed the door behind him.

I looked up in disbelief. Was this man mocking me? I felt bad enough about myself without some total stranger abusing me.

"Pardon me—are you sure you have *my* results?" I asked. "You haven't mixed them up with someone else's, have you?"

"Nope," he said as he flipped the pages back over to reveal my name on the front cover of the printed report. "Definitely yours!"

I dropped my head into my cupped hands and closed my eyes in disbelief. *How could this be true?* I thought. *I'm the village idiot. I came last in my class, term after term. What if these test results are true, and all this time, I've been lied to?*

I tasted the salty tears streaming down my face before I realised I had started to sob uncontrollably.

Are You Choosing Your Words Carefully?

Remember that old rhyme, "Sticks and stones may break my bones, but words can never hurt me." Well, it turns out that what we are saying, might, after all, be killing us!

In 2004, Dr Masaru Emoto conducted a well-known experiment that was brought to the big screen in the film *What The Bleep Do We Know?*

The experiment proves his theory that words can have a dramatic impact on the structure of water molecules. His highest profile experiment was with two jars of rice, submerged in distilled water. The first jar, with negative words written externally and spoken orally to it on a daily basis, resulted in prolific bacterial growth. By contrast, the alternative jar, which had positive words written on and spoken over it, had barely changed over the same timeframe.

As we know, our body comprises 70 percent (or more) of water. This got me thinking...if water stamped with positive words can produce a far more pleasant outcome than water stamped with dark, negative phrases, surely it is time to take control of our words?

Leaders can use their words to lift a team or crush a spirit. The choice of our words is almost as impactful as the way we say them.

As mentioned in Key #2, the level of resentment I held towards my father was blown out of all proportion. It was only after I invested in my self-development that I realised I could control our relationship and transform it into a positive one. That was accomplished when I wrote a note to my father and a separate one to my mother, asking them to forgive my behaviour. I realised I had unfairly criticised my parents for my perceptions about their shortcomings.

In short, I had behaved like a classic victim. I had spent all this time in B.E.D. (Blame, Excuses, and Denial). I had blamed my parents for their behaviour bringing me up, using my father's words as the reason for my poor performances in my personal and business lives.

As a leader, I had the tools at my disposal to turn into a victor instead. I had an O.A.R. at my disposal—Ownership, Accountability, and Responsibility.

I concluded my notes by telling my parents that I thanked them for all the things they had done for me—their unconditional love, their support, even their finances. I told them I forgave them for anything they had done to me, or that I had imagined them to have performed against me. I then signed off my notes with love, sealed the envelopes, addressed and posted them.

Take the time to identify broken relationships that have been holding you back from accomplishing things of significance. Reach out to those people and offer them olive branches of reconciliation.

To help you choose your words carefully, here are five simple things to consider to help you maximise your potential and lift your leadership to the next level:

1. Don't speak words in anger.... Ask for forgiveness and forgive the person who has offended you because unforgiveness is like drinking poison, but expecting the other person to die!
2. If you can't say something positive, don't say anything you'll regret later!
3. Try complimenting people, and make that compliment specific.
4. Make sure your words breathe life into your situation. As the old proverb says, "Death and life are in the power of the tongue, and those who love it will eat its fruits."
5. What does your T-shirt say about you? Take stock of your wardrobe and ensure that it is filled with clothes that promote positivity.

Remember to consider these five things, and use them to maximise your potential and lift your lid at all times!

Are You Employed for Your Brains or Your Brawn?

Many years ago, I read a lovely story in Jack Welch's autobiography, *Jack: Straight from the Gut.* As the CEO of G.E., one of the largest companies in the world, Welch and his team embarked on the implementation of a Six-Sigma program. In essence, it is a set of tools designed to remove defects in any process.

The program's philosophy is that everybody within the workforce has an opportunity to voice his or her opinion on how to improve any aspect of the processes used within the work environment.

During a visit to one of G.E.'s manufacturing plants in the Midwestern United States, an employee approached Welch and thanked him. After working at that plant for nearly ten years, this was the first time he had been listened to. When his suggestion was implemented, it led to an improvement in the process.

What stuck out to me was the man's comment to Welch. "I want to thank you, Mr. Welch," the employee went on to say. "For nine years you employed me for my brawn. Now you're employing me for my brain!"

Are Your Employees Solution-Focused?

During my Amway days, I remember hearing Nancy Dornan share a story that amplified the Six-Sigma point above. As mentioned in Key #4, Dornan and her husband Jim headed up an organisation called Network 21. They were a support arm to the Amway business.

The Dornans had to overcome dreadful personal circumstances when their second child Eric was born with spina bifida. It was a devastating situation that neither of them had anticipated. As a result, they had to make their Amway business successful to help them pay their ever-increasing medical bills. In addition, Jim and Nancy were determined to give their son a quality of life that would enable him to live long and productively.

Needless to say, they were my heroes, and I learned a lot from their personal story.

On one occasion, Dornan shared a story that happened when

she was travelling internationally. A staff member told her there was a problem with her ongoing travel itinerary. A busy individual, Dornan wasn't in a position to invest much more time to get this issue resolved. She was talking to large audiences all over the world.

When she quizzed her staff member on the potential solutions available, the reply identified the root cause of the problem. "I'm unsure what we can do," her assistant said.

Dornan went on to explain that she employed people to think through the issues and be solution-focused. She made it quite clear that she was expecting people to address potential problems by analysing them, identifying the potential solutions, and coming back with a series of recommended solutions.

To be honest, I was with Dornan the whole way. Why would someone come to you and say, "Hey, boss, you've got a problem, and from where I sit, it ain't looking very pretty!" It's my opinion that everything can be resolved with two resources—time and money.

When it comes to your problems, how are you and your staff tackling them? Are you solution-focused? Do you have more than one solution available? Are you working through the cost impact of alternative options to determine the best course of action to follow? Or are you simply saying, "There's a problem—*you* fix it"?

Are You Green and Growing or Ripe and Rotting?

When I was growing up in the UK, I can remember my father asking me a simple question, "Do you read books?"

My answer was emphatic, "Of course I do!"

What my dad wanted to know was whether I was reading self-development books like *The Magic of Thinking Big* by David J. Schwartz or *How to Win Friends and Influence People* by Dale Carnegie. Instead, I was reading Stephen King novels!

The reality is that whatever you are reading will eventually start to influence your thinking. Whatever you put into you will eventually have to come back out. Unfortunately, not everything that you read is potentially good for you. In the computing industry, there is a lovely acronym called GIGO. It simply stands for 'Garbage In, Garbage Out'.

What types of books are you using to help you expand your thinking? The self-help section of the library is the biggest growing section. Whether it has to do with weight loss and living a healthy lifestyle, leadership, or changing your mind-set, there is a lot of choice out there.

My journey of self-discovery started in 1998 when I was introduced to the Amway business. Irrespective of your thoughts about or experiences with the direct-selling or network marketing industry, I have to say I am grateful for my involvement. Not necessarily because I generated an income stream from it, but because of how I grew as an individual.

Books like *Personality Plus* and *The 5 Love Languages* were some of the first personal development books I read. Such books helped me to understand myself and to read the people around me. These books revolutionised my thinking. They opened my mind to the possibility that I could control my thinking and behaviour. They also took me one step further—they taught me how to interface with people. The fundamentals of these books have set the foundations of my leadership.

In addition to reading self-help books, I became an avid reader of autobiographies. I soon learned there are three ways we can learn:

1. Experience
2. Imitation
3. Reflection

Experience is by far the toughest way to learn. We often state that it is 'learning from our own mistakes.'

Imitation allows us to see what someone else has done and repeat that person's actions. Sometimes, this can also be a painful and difficult process.

Reflection is the third and most powerful method for learning. In his book, *The 15 Invaluable Laws of Growth*, John Maxwell talks about the power of pausing because reflection turns experience into insight. Maxwell says, "Experience is not the best teacher. Evaluated experience is!"

If you are spending time and money investing in your library of self-help books and programs, are you taking the time to reflect on what you are learning?

International best-selling author Jim Collins, in his book *Good to Great*, encourages us to take time to put some 'P.W.S.' into our calendar. It stands for 'Personal White Space'. When implemented, it allows you to allocate in your schedule some uninterrupted, quality time to contemplate things. Time where you have no interruptions—no cellphone, no emails, no disruptions.

Take the time to list the top 10 most influential books you have read over your lifetime. Then ask yourself, "What are the lessons I learned from these books?" Finally, be honest with yourself and document the areas of change within your life that have come as a direct result of these lessons. I think you will surprise yourself when you do this exercise.

BOOK TITLE	IMPACT ON MY LIFE

How Have You Used Information You've Learned in the Past?

When I graduated from university with my Bachelor of Science degree, I hung on to my lecture notes. Soon I was adding to them as I embarked on my Master of Science degree.

Upon graduation, I started my first full-time position as an electronic test engineer. You'll read in Key #1 that it was only six weeks after I commenced that job that I received my first promotion. Soon weeks turned into months, which turned into a year or two. My lecture notes now lay pathetically dormant, irrelevant to the job I was doing. At this point, I looked at my lecture notes and determined they were just taking up valuable real estate in my bedroom. So, with little thought, I threw them away. After all, I knew I would never need the information held there to help me with my job.

With hindsight, I realise that my actions were inaccurate and immature. You can always apply what you learn. But to realise that, you need to have a mind-set that learning doesn't stop with your formal education. When it comes to your self-development, how are you determining what is happening with the information you gathered throughout your life?

At one stage in my life, I would be reading two or three books per month. Each book came at a cost. I would allocate at least fifteen minutes per day (often at night) to read at least one chapter in the book. I would also have a highlighter in my hand, which proved to be one of the most useful reading tools I possessed.

Whenever I came across a line in a book that stood out to me, or a quote that made sense, I would highlight it. On some pages, I would take whole sections, two or three paragraphs in length, and highlight them. This technique would pay off in dividends in the future.

If I wanted to look for something to reference either in my training programs, or as an example to support a keynote I was delivering, I knew a simple flick through the book could lead me to the text of choice. Instead of having to read the whole book, my eye was drawn to the relevant sections.

To help you find books worth investing in, I have created my recommended reading list for you at the end of this book.

Applying lessons from Nelson Mandela's life:

Key #10 - LEARNING IS YOUR RESPONSIBILITY

Mandela arrived in Johannesburg in 1941. There he met Walter Sisulu. His first impression of Sisulu was that he was an educated man. Teaching in Fort Hare led Mandela to believe that proficiency in the English language, coupled with success in business, were a direct result of high academic achievements. Similarly, he assumed that Sisulu was a university graduate.

After he left Sisulu's office, Mandela was told by his cousin:

"[T]hat Walter Sisulu had never gone beyond Standard VI. It was another lesson from Fort Hare that I had to unlearn in Johannesburg. I had been taught that to have a BA meant to be a leader, and to be a leader one needed a BA."

Leaders need to be willing to further their educations beyond the boundaries of the university campus. Many of the men Mandela met in Johannesburg had not even received a school certificate! Whilst he continued his education via correspondence with UNISA (the University for South Africa), his leadership education started by surrounding himself with other thought leaders who would help to stretch his thinking. What steps are you putting in place to extend your education as a leader...?

"Education is the most powerful weapon which you can use to change the world."

— Nelson Mandela

Key #11

ALLOWING PEOPLE TO MAKE MISTAKES IS GOOD FOR YOUR BUSINESS

"Failure is instructive. The person who really thinks learns quite as much from his failures as from his successes."

— John Dewey

What I'm about to say next might shock some of you. It is OK for you or your team to make a mistake! As long as you learn from it. Learning is your responsibility. This is the key we just covered. Those of us who have children seem to spend most of our time trying to protect them from any inherent dangers. We warn them about taking care not to bump their heads or touch something sharp. Obviously, this is a sensible course of action to take. But I would like you to explore the benefits of making a mistake and *learning* from it in this key.

Are You Willing to Forgive Others?

If you were to ask people on the street what forgiveness means to them, I'm sure you would get many different answers. Some might say it's a willingness to pardon someone for something that person did or said to you. Others might define it as a process by which a victim undergoes a change in attitude or feelings which resulted from an offense inflicted upon them. It might even be a willingness to let go of negative emotions toward someone, such as vengeance.

The truth is that, at some point in time, an offence can occur, and sometimes, it can be the result of a mistake that was made.

Forgiveness does not condone the offense or act, but the person who forgives may gain the ability to wish the offender well. For the offended person, it could be giving up the right to hurt those who have hurt you. We can say we forgive and forget, but can we really forget? It is possible to forgive, but is it humanly possible to forget? Not likely.

As a man of faith, I am drawn to the biblical definition of forgiveness. It is a much broader and more comprehensive definition than what the world believes. For most Christians, the words of 'The Lord's Prayer' will ring loud in our ears when we think of forgiveness. In this scripture, found in Matthew 6:9-13, Jesus shows us what forgiveness really is: "Forgive us our trespasses [mistakes or sins] as we forgive others who trespass [sin or offend] against us."

Jesus went on to summarise the value of forgiveness by stating, in Matthew 6:14, "For if you forgive others their trespasses, your heavenly Father will also forgive you."

This principle also applies in business. One such instance came to my attention when a business colleague started collating a list of people who had offended him in the past whom he was unwilling to forgive. If you have been in business for any length of time, I am sure you have committed at least one mistake during your career. How would you like to find your name on someone's list?

Jesus was once asked if a woman, who was caught in the act of adultery, should be stoned to death—as was prescribed by Jewish law. Jesus responded, "Let him who is without sin cast the first stone." Soon the adulterous woman was left by herself as the crowd dispersed, convicted by Jesus' words. None of us has led a guilt-free or mistake-free life. We are all guilty of making a mistake. The only question for any of us to ask is, "Have I learned from that mistake?"

John Maxwell wrote a book titled *Sometimes You Win; Sometimes You Learn*. Its premise is that any setback, whether professional or personal, can be turned into a step forward when you possess the right tools to turn a loss into a gain.

As a leader, you must allow your team members to make mistakes and to understand that they live in a positive and nurturing environment where they will be supported through their learning process. Learning is not easy during down times; it takes discipline to do the right thing when something goes wrong. Maxwell often points out that experience isn't the best teacher; evaluated experience is. I encourage you to take the same viewpoint.

Are You Learning from Someone Else's Mistakes?

Social media has brought us even closer to each other. Today, it is becoming alarmingly difficult for you to post something that doesn't have a chance of going viral.

When I was in the U.S., speaking at a conference in Stamford, Connecticut in October 2014, our keynote speaker, Des Hague, opened the conference by sharing a timely tale of his misfortune at the hands of social media. Its power became apparent when a video obtained from the CCTV footage from a Vancouver hotel elevator went viral. Hague was the CEO of the U.S. catering company Centerplate when he was caught on camera kicking a small, cowering dog five times and swinging it up from the ground by its leash.

Hague pleaded guilty to animal cruelty and resigned from Centerplate. He was ordered by the company to donate $100,000 to animal welfare following the public furore over the August 2014 incident.

Today, it is estimated that a cosmopolitan city like London will have in excess of 500,000 cameras in operation in public places. Data captured in 2014 showed that in New Zealand, Auckland Transport's network alone included 2,500 cameras on bus, ferry, rail, and road networks. Hundreds of others dot retail and recreation centres across the city.

As a leader, you need to ensure that you are always on the right side of the law. This applies to both your public as well as private persona. It is no longer taken for granted that a home is a man's castle. Are you the type of leader who is the same person at work as you are at home?

Do You Wish Children Came with a User's Manual?

Put your hand up if you have children.

Keep your hand up if you wish they came with a user's manual!

Chances are that most of us wish we could have had a manual when our children were growing up. If you have yet to start a family, or your child is still an infant or toddler, you will soon be wishing that this fictitious manual existed!

The practical truth is that you have to learn how to bring up a child. According to UCLA research from 2005, a child will hear the word 'no' more than 400 times in a day! 'No' can become the default response from a parent attempting to protect his or her child from a potentially life-threatening situation.

But it is also proven that children will learn from their mistakes.

According to an article by Jennifer Shakeel, our attempts as parents to shield our children from making mistakes can be detrimental to their development. Shakeel says:

> Although we as parents often wish to shield our child from the frustration and disappointment of making mistakes, it's important to realize that making mistakes is part of an important learning process in life. No matter how hard we might try to always do things right, making mistakes is one thing that is always part of life, regardless of whether we are young or old. It is important to teach a child that making a mistake isn't fatal, and that they can use mistakes as a way of learning to find better ways to be successful.

As a leader, do you apply the same principle to your team members? Are you encouraging them to take calculated risks and to grow? Do you provide them with that safety net within your organisation? Do you take them through a debrief once a mistake has been identified that empowers them to learn, or do you create an atmosphere of retribution?

How you handle mistakes and failure creates an important cultural expectation that can attract or repel people. Take the time to list the mistakes you or your colleagues have made and the learning lessons that have come out of those experiences:

MISTAKE	LEARNING LESSON

What Wisdom Do We Learn from Our Ancestors?

At the ripe old age of fifteen, I was driven back to my boarding school by my father. He pulled up his champagne-coloured Cortina Mark IV outside of the entrance to my house and then handed me a small white box, saying, "Give this to your house-master."

"What's in the box?" I enquired.

"Kahek and Mahmoul," he replied. These are special cakes that the Greeks prepare to celebrate Easter.

"Why should I give them to him?" I asked.

"You never know when you might need to curry favour from him," my dad stated.

"I'll *never* need his help," I spat back at my father. "I'll know everything that I need to know!" And *that* was when I learned my first lesson in life: It's not what you know, but who you know that makes a difference.

We will all make mistakes. How we respond to them and grow from them becomes an important aspect of our personal growth. Maxwell identifies humility as one of the spirits of learning. Author Jim Collins, a self-professed student of companies—great ones, good ones, weak ones and failed ones—wrote in *How the Mighty Fall* about the catastrophic failure of Motorola in the mid-1990s.

"Motorola's magnificent run of success which culminated in having grown from $5 billion to $27 billion in annual revenues in just a decade, contributed to a cultural shift from humility to arrogance...."

"Hubris," Collins continues, "is defined as excessive pride that brings down a hero."

Collins goes on to describe the success of Wal-Mart. Identified at #1 on the Fortune 500 list with $379 billion in annual revenues back in 2008, Collins attributes its success to Sam Walton's deep humility and learning orientation. Walton was the only CEO from a list of ten American retailing companies to accept a request to host a group of Brazilian investors, intent on learning how to run their new company better. With most of the questioning emanating from Walton, as he stood over the kitchen sink washing and drying dishes after dinner, it became evident that he sought to learn from them, not the other way around!

What lessons can we, as leaders, learn from Sam Walton and the Wal-Mart story? I would suggest we learn that our positions or titles do not make us successful leaders. This mistake has been made by too many high profile leaders who have preceded us. Collins concludes that the real learning for businesses is that, like Wal-Mart, a business should not exist for the aggrandisement of it leaders; it exists for its customers.

Applying lessons from Nelson Mandela's life:

Key #11 - ALLOWING PEOPLE TO MAKE MISTAKES IS GOOD FOR YOUR BUSINESS

Using his expertise as a lawyer, Mandela would often represent other prisoners. It was a way they could stand up to the authorities. One day, he heard that another inmate, called Bogart, had been savagely beaten by a warder. Although Mandela had not witnessed the assault, the cuts and bruises on the victim's face provided enough evidence.

Having previously seen the benefit of his petition on behalf of another prisoner who had been assaulted (the warder in question was transferred off the island), Mandela immediately demanded to see the commanding officer.

The following day, the commander blandly informed Mandela that the case had been investigated and dismissed. Bogart, it appeared, had denied that he was ever assaulted.

Mandela claimed that was impossible since he had spoken to Bogart only the day before. At that point, a lieutenant led Bogart into the room. His face was covered with bandages. When the commander asked him whether or not he had been beaten, Bogart said quietly, 'No, baas,' without meeting Mandela's gaze. 'I was never assaulted.' He was then dismissed.

Mandela makes the following observation in his book: "[T]he commander said, 'the case is closed.' The commander had succeeded in humiliating me. He had obviously bribed Bogart with extra food and tobacco to drop his charges. From that point on, I demanded a signed and written statement from a prisoner before I agreed to take up his case."

Mandela had learned an important lesson from his mistake, and he ensured that he didn't repeat it. As a leader, your ability to learn from your mistakes is important. But even more so is your ability to allow your followers to make mistakes, knowing they live in a supportive environment. Otherwise, you may find yourself walking on a lonely and deserted road....

"Especially for those of us who lived in single cells, you had the time to sit down and think, and we discovered that sitting down just to think is one of the best ways of keeping yourself fresh and able, to be able to address the problems facing you, and you had the opportunity, also, of examining your past."

— Nelson Mandela

Key #12

NURTURING RELATIONSHIPS WITH KEY PEOPLE

"Truth is everybody is going to hurt you:
you just gotta find the ones worth suffering for."

— Bob Marley

Now that we've discussed how to develop key relationships with people you can trust and why you should allow them to make and learn from their own mistakes, in this next key, we'll explore nurturing those relationships. Once you have established a link with somebody, how are you going to invest in that person? Similar to the story about a fictitious bank account that you deposit funds into each time you do something nice for someone, your key relationships will respond to you based on their current bank balances. The more you do for somebody, the larger the surplus becomes. But the flip side is that you can quickly deplete those reserves by letting people down. This key explores how you can keep that bank balance in the black.

Are You Investing in Others?

When I was a senior consultant, I had the privilege of working under an incredible leader. She was a driven and focussed individual who had an incredibly compassionate side to her.

Despite the number of direct reports she had in her team, she made it a priority to have a one-on-one with each individual. We would meet up at least once a month, and each meeting had focus and purpose.

With every get-together, she would start the conversation by asking about my family. She knew my wife and was always interested in her welfare and how my kids were doing. For me, this was a breath of fresh air! Somebody who put family above work was a rarity in the corporate world.

When the conversation changed to work, she would always ask deep and meaningful questions. Nothing was taken for granted. I was made to think through my answers, and it taught me a lesson—always arrive prepared.

Her technique was one of inclusiveness. She would allow me to share my thoughts, and then we would explore them together. There was no pre-judgement, and the conversation always led us to some level of discovery.

On the occasions when I had made a mistake (and yes, it is important to acknowledge that you *are* allowed to make mistakes), she had a wonderful way of taking you through the lesson. At the end of the day, her view was simply this—allow people to learn from their mistakes. Otherwise, they will continue to repeat them and, worse still, make even bigger ones later on.

How often do you get together with your key people? Are you able to take them through a journey of discovery? Will they grow as a result of spending time with you, or are you more likely to tear a strip off them (especially if they make mistakes)?

She was able to get more out of me and the rest of her team because she was willing to invest in us. By the end of each meeting, she would keep a written list of the topics discussed and the action items agreed upon. It was my responsibility to do the same. For me, the task was made easier because of the relationship. Even though I considered her a friend, we always respected that distinction of leader and follower.

I was so impressed with her leadership style that I delivered a handwritten thank-you note to her when I exited her department. A year later, I happened to visit her. To my surprise, my note was still attached to her office wall. And that got me thinking....

When Was the Last Time You Handwrote a Card?

In 1999, I had the privilege of running a call centre here in New Zealand. We were the 'As Seen on TV' company. My team was responsible for answering the calls that flooded in after the infomercials ran on TV. Due to the volume of calls we received, we would need to get all hands on deck just to ensure we didn't lose too many because of lengthy call queue times.

One particular product we had was so popular that we needed to get help from every department. With the blessing of the other department heads, we arranged training for staff members who came in to help from our warehouse, retail centre, and accounting department. Training was intense, but effective.

The onslaught was concentrated, and the staff absorbed the calls over the hour-long period. Considering the lack of exposure many of our helpers had to call handling, they all did an exceptional job. The chatter was audible as they departed the floor and returned to their 'day jobs'. Giggles were heard as they high-fived my team in recognition of their accomplishments.

That evening, I took the time to write out personal handwritten messages to each volunteer. Late into the night, I completed my task by addressing their envelopes, delivering them to their desks where they would receive them in the morning.

Early the following day, I returned to the office to catch up with my administrative tasks. With my head bowed down, focussed on the task at hand, I never saw the person heading towards my office. My first sense of her impending arrival was through the tremors that her purposeful and determined steps brought to my office.

I looked up in time to see her walk through my open door. With a resolute shove, she closed my office door behind her. Tears had already welled up in her eyes, and she didn't need an invitation from me to sit down. I was concerned that I had done something unintentional to offend her, so I asked whether there was anything I could do.

Through her tears, she confessed that the note I had written to thank her for contributing to our successes the previous day had touched her on a deep and profound level. In nearly twenty years of working, she had never received a note that thanked her for her contributions!

Little did I know this simple gesture could have an intense effect on others.

What have you done recently to acknowledge someone's contribution? When did you last handwrite a personal note of thanks and gratitude to a colleague? How did you feel the last time you received a handwritten letter through the post?

PEOPLE I HAVE TO RECOGNISE	REASON

Are You Aware of Who Knows You?

Receiving acknowledgement for your work can positively improve your outlook. I was the recipient of acknowledgement for my work, but it didn't come from the source I would have expected.

I am lucky enough to hold dual nationality. When I was living in the UK, I needed to renew my Greek passport, so I ventured into the Greek Embassy in London. After a short while, a member of the staff approached me and asked me whether I was Greek. With my limited knowledge of the Greek language, I explained that I was and that I had come to renew my passport.

Ushered to the front of the queue, I was seated next to a lovely lady who helped me with my enquiry. However, it soon became apparent that we had a problem. I was asked where my military service papers were. Having been born in North Africa and lived in the UK since 1970, I had never served my compulsory military service. I explained that my father had previously taken care of that for me.

At that point, I made my excuses and left the Embassy. When I got home, I called my father, who was holidaying in Crete that summer. He proceeded to tell me off and gave me specific instructions not to return to the Embassy before his return to London.

A few weeks later, we both returned to the Greek Embassy. My father held a briefcase in his hand, which I assumed had the appropriate paperwork within it. We were greeted by the staff, who obviously knew my father by sight. They led us to the front of the queue where we were re-engaged by the same lady I had spoken to earlier.

Formal greetings were completed with hugs and kisses on each cheek because my father and the official were on first name terms. After the pleasantries were concluded, my father entered into business mode.

For my benefit, the conversation returned to English and my father proceeded to open his briefcase and extract a manila envelope. He carefully removed a number of newspaper clippings which he arranged across the table.

"These are press clippings of my son," my father proudly explained. I had no idea he had been collecting them!

"Do you know who my son is? Here he is in the *Daily Telegraph*. There's an article in the *Sunday Times*, about my son. Here he is with the Duke of Westminster, doing a product launch with the Deaf Society. My son knows the Duke of Westminster. Heck, I suspect that he knows the Prince of Wales and probably the Queen herself!"

At that point, the official pulled my passport towards her with her left hand, and with her right hand, she proceeded to stamp my passport and renew it for a further ten years—no questions asked!

My father taught me many lessons on how to engage with key people. He had a great sense of authority, and even though he had retired from his job as a bank officer in his early fifties, he carried an air of influence. From an early age, I observed his ability to connect with people. He always smiled, and his smile was infectious. His desire to find out more about others and, in particular, key facts about their personal lives was a lesson in engagement I would never forget.

He taught me that leaders touch a heart before they ask for a hand.

Are You Big Enough to Say Hello?

Over the years, I have been blessed to know many magnificent leaders and accomplished businesspeople. One of the nicest people I ever met was my upline Double Diamond, Glenda Leonard.

She is one of the most successful businesswomen I ever knew. My wife and I had the privilege of hosting her during some of her many visits to New Zealand. Glenda was approachable and kind-hearted. Her knowledge of the Amway business was second to none. More importantly, she had a way of encouraging people to come out of their shells and contribute to the benefit of the wider team.

By the middle of 2006, Kay and I decided to step back from actively building our Amway business. It was something we had discussed at some length with our frontline Diamonds, Simon and Yvonne Godfrey. We were in need of a sabbatical, and we received their blessing.

During a business trip to Sydney later that year, I entered the hotel lobby with a dozen of my Kiwi colleagues. As we walked towards the reception area to check in, I saw three ladies sitting in armchairs to the side of the room and engaged in deep conversation. Immediately, I recognised Glenda and I could see she was in the middle of a counselling session.

I pulled up to the side of the chairs and stood to quiet attention about two metres away from them. I waited patiently, and soon, Glenda looked up and recognised me. She interrupted her conversation, graciously stood up, and calling me by name, gave me a big hug! Not wanting to interrupt her counselling session, I simply told her that I had wanted to say hello to her.

Glenda reassured me that she was happy to see me and took a few minutes to focus her complete attention on me. I found out she was already aware of our decision to take a sabbatical. She supported that decision and reassured me that although we would be missed from the business meetings, she understood our motivation.

My business colleagues were astounded that I knew Glenda. It was obvious from her outward appearance that she was a wealthy and successful person. When I told them she was probably in the top ten businesswomen by revenue in Australia at the time, they were taken aback. None of them could comprehend how somebody that important and wealthy would interrupt a conversation just to say hello to someone.

As a leader, are you taking the time to nurture your relationships with key people? Do you know enough about them that you can connect with them at a heart and not just a head level? Are you willing to invest in key people who might be three or four levels deep within your organisation?

Take the time to go through the key movers and shakers within your organisation and list the people whom you believe make a contribution to the company's growth and profitability. Make a determined effort to set aside time to get to know them and get them to understand how you can contribute to their personal development.

If you stay aloof, then you risk the chance of alienating them from you and your organisation. But, like Glenda, you might be able to touch someone's heart and get even more out of him or her. On a personal level, I think we accomplished more within our Amway business as a direct result of Glenda's kindness and sincere interest in us and our success.

KEY MOVERS AND SHAKERS	ACTION WITH THAT PERSON

What Languages Do You Speak?

When I lived in the UK, I returned home one day after a successful meeting with the head of I.T. with a leading bank. As I entered the house, I said to my girlfriend at the time, "Sweetheart—I'm home!" I expected her to chime out, "Honey, you're my hero!" Instead, I heard a hoarse voice growl back at me, "Your dinner's ready. Go and throw the rubbish out!"

To say I was discouraged must have been the biggest understatement. These dialogues led to frustration on both sides. I was expecting her to tell me constantly how good I was, and she was always asking me to tidy up behind me. We soon drifted apart and separated.

Over a decade later, I found myself living in New Zealand. I had entered into a new relationship, but I was starting to see the same patterns repeating themselves. It was as though I had started to live in my own version of the classic film *Groundhog Day*! I recognised the symptoms, but I didn't have the code to unlock the mystery.

During a coffee with one of my good friends, I mentioned my dilemma in passing. He looked me square in the eyes and confessed that he had no idea what made women tick. The best he could do was recommend that I read *The 5 Love Languages* by Gary Chapman.

This book revolutionised my thinking about the way we communicate with others. In his book, Chapman states, "Falling in love is easy. Staying in love—that's the challenge! How can you keep your relationship fresh and growing amid the demands, conflicts, and just plain boredom of everyday life?"

If you haven't read Chapman's book, may I be bold enough to encourage you to make it an urgent priority for both your personal life and your business prosperity.

Chapman claims there are five dominant ways we can communicate with others. In a nutshell, they are:

1. Words of Affirmation
2. Acts of Service
3. Receiving Gifts
4. Quality Time
5. Physical Touch

After reading his book, I realised my main love language was 'Words of Affirmation'. I was always saying things similar to, "I love you!" "Well done!" or "You're the best!" I was the main cheerleader for the team, and I knew how to bring the best out of people. In return, that was exactly what I wanted to hear people reply back to me.

I then realised that when I was given an instruction to take the rubbish out, or to go mow the lawn, it was the language of a person who was seeking 'Acts of Service'. If only I had realised that we were simply talking different languages!

Over time, I started to recognise the languages of the people surrounding me. One of my daughters would go to the beach, find a shell that she would bring home, wrap it in tissue paper, and then give it to me. It was a gift! She spoke the third language.

My mother, on the other hand, would get upset with me on her birthday. Even though we lived at opposite ends of the world, I would always remember to call her on that day. But she would sob uncontrollably, citing a lack of a birthday card as proof that I didn't love her. On examination, I found out that she thought that if I had spent the time hunting down the perfect card for her, handwriting the note, and posting it to arrive on time, then I would have spent the 'quality time' on her that she was seeking. Isn't it funny how other people think? Obviously, my mother spoke the fourth language.

The final love language, physical touch, is the easiest to recognise. When people who speak this language enter a room, they even give hugs to strangers! My son was a classic 'physical touch' speaker. He would often offer to give you a shoulder massage, or would hold your hand whilst walking on the beach. To make him feel loved, I would often run my hand through his hair. Well, why wouldn't I—after all, he *has* hair!

What do the Five Love Languages have to do with leadership? Everything!

Whilst Chapman wrote them with marriage in mind, I believe the principles extend out to the business world as well.

If you think about the people you spend most of your time with, you will probably start to recognise these five languages in their everyday behaviour. There is the person who offers to get a coffee for everyone in the office, the person who is giving high-fives as he goes past you, and the person who gives handwritten notes of encouragement. The list goes on....

Take the time to write down two lists—one of the top five people you interact with in business, and one of your spouse and four closest family members. Spend some time figuring out which love language each person speaks the loudest. I think you'll be surprised what you find out.

PEOPLE I WORK WITH										
NAME	WORDS OF AFFIRMATION		ACTS OF SERVICE		RECEIVING GIFTS		QUALITY TIME		PHYSICAL TOUCH	
	YES	*NO*	*YES*	*NO*	*YES*	*NO*	*YES*	*NO*	*YES*	*NO*

SPOUSE AND FOUR CLOSEST FAMILY MEMBERS										
NAME	WORDS OF AFFIRMATION		ACTS OF SERVICE		RECEIVING GIFTS		QUALITY TIME		PHYSICAL TOUCH	
	YES	*NO*	*YES*	*NO*	*YES*	*NO*	*YES*	*NO*	*YES*	*NO*

Applying lessons from Nelson Mandela's life:

Key #12 - NURTURING RELATIONSHIPS WITH KEY PEOPLE

Mandela was a well-read man. Despite the limited library at

Robben Island, Mandela was drawn to one book in particular that he returned to many times. It was Tolstoy's greatest work, *War and Peace*. Mandela was interested in the character of General Kutuzov, whom everyone at the Russian court underestimated.

Mandela commented: "Kutuzov defeated Napoleon precisely because he was not swayed by the ephemeral and superficial values of the court, and made his decisions on a visceral understanding of his men and his people. It reminded me once again that truly to lead one's people one must also truly know them."

This mind-set embodies this leadership key. To get the best out of your team or your people, you truly need to know them. Live this leadership key and know that you will walk confidently down the road because others will have your back....

"If you talk to a man in a language he understands, that goes to his head. If you talk to him in his language, that goes to his heart."

— Nelson Mandela

Key #13

OVERCOMING OBSTACLES

"Success is to be measured not so much by the position that one has reached in life as by the obstacles which he has overcome."

— Booker T. Washington

By now, as a leader, you are surrounded by people you can trust, whom you are investing in and whom you know more deeply. If this were a perfect world, we would stop here and all live happily ever after. But the reality is that life happens, and to quote Forrest Gump, "Life is like a box of chocolates. You never know what you're gonna get." Issues will arise, and obstacles will need to be overcome. How you handle them determines how effective you will be as a leader.

What Lessons Can You Learn from Your Mother?

I'm an avid reader of autobiographies. I particularly like to read about successful entrepreneurs or political figures who have changed the world.

One of the most inspirational books I have read is Richard

Branson's *Losing My Virginity*. His story of overcoming obstacles started at an early age. There is a rather well-known story about Branson being dropped off by his mum on the way home from a shopping trip. He was only five years old, and they were approximately five kilometres from home. Branson was told to find his own way home.

In a blog on the Virgin website, titled 'Richard Branson: 5 lessons from my Mum', Branson says, "She was punishing me for causing mischief in the back seat, but she was also teaching me a larger lesson about overcoming my disabling shyness and learning to ask others for directions."

I like that Branson refers to the following five lessons his mother taught him over his life:

1. Live with no regrets
2. Learn to survive—fast
3. Put others first
4. Keep your feet on the ground
5. Every day is a fresh chance

In his explanation of the first point, he says, "I'm often flabbergasted by the amount of time some people waste dwelling on their past failures, rather than directing that energy into new projects. My mother always taught me never to look back in regret, but to immediately move on to the next thing."

We will always have obstacles to overcome. John Maxwell wrote an exceptional book about dealing with obstacles titled *Sometimes You Win, Sometimes You Learn*. I am in total agreement with both Maxwell and Branson that you should never look back with regret. It's one technique you can develop to help you grow as a leader.

Are Obstacles Limiting Your Progress?

Cash flow is one of the biggest contributors to businesses' demises. My thinking about cash flow was dramatically alerted by a presentation from Jentezen Franklin.

Franklin is the Pastor of Free Chapel, in Gainesville, Georgia, with a congregation of 10,000 in weekly attendance. I was privileged to hear him present to a business audience here in New Zealand in 2010. It coincided with the birth of my business. I had my 'Lifting the Lid' program running on the same day, so even though cash flow was tight, I decided to invest in having my clients attend his session.

Franklin taught on the four Bs that affect our finances:

1. Bag
2. Bowl
3. Baskets
4. Barn

He used biblical stories to illustrate each B.

For the first 'B', BAG, he told the story of Judas, one of the twelve apostles who followed Jesus Christ during his life on earth. Judas was in charge of the money, but he spent all his time holding tightly to the moneybag. In John 12, when a woman bought expensive oil to anoint Jesus, Judas complained about what he perceived as a waste of money. Holding too tightly to your money, however, ultimately leads to a poverty mentality. When you hold the bag shut all the time, the money will eventually rub a hole in the fabric and fall out of the bottom of your bag. In this case, you will never have enough money.

The second story was about the widow and the BOWL, found in 2 Kings 4. Franklin shared how with one small bowl of oil, the widow and her sons were persuaded by the Prophet Elijah to ask all the neighbours for their empty jugs. She then started to pour the oil out of the bowl. It filled up jug after jug to the brim until they reached the last jug in the room. Only then did the oil run out as they filled that jug to the brim. This story represents having just enough money.

The third story was about the BASKETS. In the story, found in Matthew 14, Jesus miraculously feeds 5,000 people with just five loaves of bread and two fish. After blessing the food and breaking it up for distribution amongst the crowd, the disciples gather up twelve baskets of leftover food. With this story, Franklin points out, we have moved from not enough, to just enough, and then to more than enough.

Finally, Franklin commented on the story of Joseph in Genesis 14. Joseph interprets Pharaoh's dream of seven fat cows being eaten by the seven skinny cows as a prediction of a famine coming to the land. Joseph then builds BARNS to hold the grain that will stave off hunger and famine for the nation of Egypt. This is a story of abundance.

Each story involves obstacles of one form or another.

Judas didn't want to waste money, and he was angry that an expensive jar of alabaster oil, worth a year's wages, was broken to anoint Jesus before he was killed. His mind-set became an obstacle to spending the money which he wanted to use for the poor.

The widow was left with debt from her late husband, and the only way forward she could see was to sell her sons off to pay his debt.

The disciples had no food or money at hand, yet they had a large crowd that needed feeding.

Pharaoh had no plan to overcome the famine soon to devastate his nation and no immediate idea what his dream was.

What obstacles are you having to overcome in your life that are holding you back from accomplishing more in life? How can you turn those obstacles into opportunities for abundance in your life?

Are Obstacles Making You Stronger?

One of my mentors was the managing director and founding partner of a company where I once worked. I enjoyed my interactions with him. On the odd occasion, we would go out on prospecting calls together.

Acting as his chauffeur, I took the opportunity to ask him questions and listen to his wisdom. He was a captive audience as far as I was concerned. However, it became quite apparent that there were two camps emerging within the company—one with the managing director and the other with the sales director.

In the middle of the week, around lunchtime, the other senior managers and I were ushered into the boardroom. We were given little explanation, merely the instruction to attend this meeting.

Nervous tension filled the room as people shuffled for seats around the boardroom table. Then our CEO entered the room, accompanied by the sales director. Silence filled the room as he spoke in sombre tones. His message was short and simple. Our managing director was no longer with the company as the result of something (undisclosed) that had occurred. His dismissal was effective immediately.

We were then asked whether anyone in the room had an issue with that.

What was I supposed to say? Yes, I had an issue—I had shackled my horse to the wrong cart.

This announcement had significant ramifications for my career within that company. When you have to deal with a significant obstacle to your career, and you see a power-play evolve in front of your eyes, what are your options? As a fan of the TV show *Survivor*, I love seeing the interaction between people as they arrive for a tribal council. They have to vote a member of the tribe off, and a lot of background work occurs as alliances are formed and broken in real time.

The ultimate scheming of the contestants, who are looking to win $1 million, can lead to a 'blindsided' vote. To me, hearing about the departure of our M.D. felt like a blindside. My alliance had crumbled. Was I the next person to go? I certainly felt vulnerable with a target on my back as the result of my previous alliance.

As a leader, you will need to understand how to manoeuvre through these kinds of obstacles. Are you building bridges to others, or are you more likely to burn bridges?

Are You Setting an Extra Seat at the Table for an Unexpected Guest?

Back in Key #1, I mentioned that I became involved in the Family Party, a Christian political party that contested the 2008 General Election in New Zealand. A few months before the election, we were invited to attend the annual conference called New Zealand Forum on the Family.

Because it was an election year, this forum focussed on the issues that affected Kiwi families. Anti-smacking legislation had recently been passed that made corporal punishment of children a criminal offense. The new law was introduced against public opinion, with over 85 percent of the voting public opposing this legislation.

The debate was intense, and as one of the Christian parties represented at the election, it was expected that our party would contribute to the debate. However, when it came time to stand up and be counted, we were told that our leader—Richie Lewis—would not be given a seat at the debating table.

What I experienced was a master class on leadership as Lewis approached the organisers before the session to ask why he couldn't participate. A number of obstacles were put up, most of them centered around another participant joining the panel at such a late stage.

Lewis then made a comment that changed the game: "You know that you always set out a place at the dining table for an unexpected guest—that's a Christian thing to do. Would you deny somebody food at your feast?"

His leadership shone through that day. He was given a seat at the table and an opportunity to be heard.

What do you do as a leader to get your voice heard? Do you try to bash down the door, or simply turn around and walk away from the locked door? Obstacles are put in front of you to help you grow your character and develop the leader within.

How Many People Do You Know?

When I arrived in New Zealand in 1995, apart from my immediate family, I only knew two recruitment consultants whom I had met in London. In a nation of 3.63 million, that wasn't a lot of people.

I was trying to establish myself in a new country, with no track history to lean on. I didn't have any financial history, which made renting appliances a challenge. I had to rent a house and wait for my furniture to arrive from the UK.

With only $15,000 to my name, I wanted to minimise the items I had to purchase, so rental seemed like a viable alternative. Unfortunately, I had no credit reference for the company to use to approve my application. It made no difference that I could point to a clean credit history from the UK—that was irrelevant in New Zealand.

Leadership is similar. No matter what you have accomplished

in another organisation, when you join a new company, you are starting from scratch. What can you do to establish your credibility with a new group of employees? How can you gain their trust and establish your credentials? What are you willing to do to gain the authority to lead from the front?

To Whom Are You Comparing Yourself?

In this day and age, a lot of information makes the rounds. One of the best ways to find out what people are thinking about you is simply to ask Mr Google. I challenge you to type your name in the Google search bar and see what comes back.

We can become obsessed with how many people like our Facebook post or comment on a LinkedIn post we have created. Social media seems to be taking hold of us and crafting our images of self-worth.

On social media, it is easy to see the exploits of your good friends. Their posts can portray them at a high level of accomplishment, which may be an inflated viewpoint they have created. Unfortunately, it's a big temptation for us to compare ourselves to others.

Pastor Paul Scanlon helped me put this all into perspective when he warned me, "Don't compare your Chapter 1 with someone else's Chapter 10!"

You have no way to know where someone else is at with his or her individual journey. Yet how often are you guilty of comparing yourself to your neighbours? We all know what it is to measure ourselves against the 'keeping up with the Joneses' indicator. We measure somebody else from an external viewpoint. Their wealth is judged by external features such as the car they drive or the 'toys' they have.

The true wealth of a leader, however, is determined by his or her character and integrity. And if you really want to know the depth of a leader, ask one to describe the obstacles he or she has overcome. That's the true measure of a leader!

Take a few minutes to document some of the obstacles you have overcome in your life:

OBSTACLES I HAVE OVERCOME

Applying lessons from Nelson Mandela's life:

Key #13 - OVERCOMING OBSTACLES

Prison life is about routine. Mandela notes that anything that departs from the pattern upsets the authorities, for routine is a sign of a well-run prison.

A particular challenge every prisoner faces is to survive intact, to emerge undiminished. To survive, he must know the enemy's purpose before adopting a strategy to undermine it. Once he understands how the authorities are operating, he has to share that with his fellow prisoners.

Sometimes as a leader, Mandela made choices and took actions that, whilst initially viewed as unpopular, had results that would not be known for years to come.

Mandela supplied the following commentary: "There are victories whose glory lies only in the fact that they are known to those who win them. This is particularly true of prison, where you must find consolation in being true to your ideals, even if no one else knows it."

As a prisoner, Mandela had to battle an enemy who was trying to break him and his spirit on a daily basis. He had to stay true to his ideals, and he had to dig deep to accomplish this. By knowing his 'Why', he could overcome any obstacle in his path....

"I am fundamentally an optimist. Whether that comes from nature or nurture, I cannot say. Part of being optimistic is keeping one's head pointed toward the sun, one's feet moving forward. There were many dark moments when my faith in humanity was sorely tested, but I would not and could not give myself up to despair. That way lay defeat and death."

— Nelson Mandela

Key #14

DEVELOPING GOOD DAILY HABITS

"Your beliefs become your thoughts,
Your thoughts become your words,
Your words become your actions,
Your actions become your habits,
Your habits become your values,
Your values become your destiny."

— Mahatma Gandhi

I mentioned that I am a man of faith. I would not be true to myself if I didn't explore the role my faith has had on my leadership journey. It is not my intention to force my faith upon you, so if you feel you might be offended, please skip through this key. However, I would encourage you at least to explore it and save your judgement until the end of this key.

When Do You Get Your Biggest Breakthroughs?

"Do you know what B.I.B.L.E. stands for?" someone once asked me. "It stands for 'Best Instruction Before Leaving Earth'!"

As a young boy, I listened to the various stories from the Bible: Samson and Delilah, Jonah and the Big Fish, Moses parting the Red Sea, Jesus feeding the five thousand.

Despite growing up in a Christian household, at the tender age of fifteen, I made a decision to walk away from God and my relationship with Him. (You can read more about that in Key #18.) For nearly thirty years, I walked in the wilderness, relying on my own strength for the decisions I made and the results I obtained. The sad truth is that if I had been measured on my performance as you would be for a test, I would have failed!

In 2005, I was led back to the Lord, and it would be remiss of me not to expand on the impact it has had on my life. One of the first things I was told after I gave my life to the Lord was that there were three things I needed to consider:

1. **I needed to talk to God on a regular basis:** Some would call it prayer, but the concept was similar to having an everyday conversation with your best friend. I was encouraged to start talking and sharing.

2. **God needed to talk to me:** One way God could talk to me was through His word, as written in the Bible. I was encouraged to read it, starting with the Gospel of Matthew in the New Testament. I was also encouraged to listen for that still, quiet voice that sometimes whispers in my ear.

3. **I was encouraged to go to church on a regular basis:** Like a newborn baby, I would need to find some shelter—a roof over my head. Church could provide me with that, and I was encouraged to find a good church near where I lived.

I concluded that I could do myself no harm by reading the Bible from cover to cover. After all, I might read something that could help me in my personal relationships or with my work. It was well worth the effort.

I was also told to read my Bible using the S.O.A.P. methodology.

S.O.A.P. stands for:

- Scripture
- Observation
- Application
- Prayer

As I started to implement Bible-reading as a daily habit, I found myself thinking through things and gaining alternative insights. It seemed that the closer I got to God, the bigger the breakthrough I was making.

What Do You Hear in the Quiet Moments?

Do you ever get that feeling that you just heard someone call you, but when you look around, you find yourself all alone? Or a random thought crosses your mind to connect with someone, who then calls you a few moments later?

I am sure we can all recall a number of instances when we have had these experiences. They probably happen more often than we are willing to admit. As a man of faith, I've realised that these whispers are the voice of God talking to me through the Holy Spirit. Given the amount of white noise that surrounds us on a daily basis, it can sometimes be quite difficult to hear that voice.

We all have different ways to enter into the zone that helps us to hear that voice. For some people, it is by going for a walk on the beach, or out in the bush, admiring God's creation. For others, it is through intense reading of His word, with a concordance to guide you on the meaning of the words. Some get to hear it during worship. Whatever the mechanism you choose, I encourage you to find out what works best for you.

If you've watched the classic Disney film, *Pinocchio*, you may remember the character of Jiminy Cricket. He became the conscience of little Pinocchio as he wandered away from his wood-carving father, Geppetto. The character's name is said to be a play on the exclamation "Jiminy Cricket!", a minced oath for "Jesus Christ." What if we did have a conscience that was, in fact, Jesus Christ himself?

How would your life improve if the maker of heaven and earth had a direct line to you? What could your life look like if you were to lean not on your own understanding, but instead, you gave up all your big problems to someone who had *all* the answers? What if you had your own 'cosmic Magic 8 Ball' that got it right every time? What question would you ask?

QUESTIONS YOU WOULD ASK THE 'COSMIC MAGIC 8 BALL'

What Is on Your Wish List?

Attention to detail doesn't rank very highly on my list of God-given talents. I'm a strategic thinker, and I can see the big picture. I might even be described as a visionary, but figuring out the minutia for that vision can bog me down.

Many leaders are great at vision casting, and they know how to sell the dreams. If you relate to that, then you will also notice that as a leader, your attention to detail might benefit from some further refinement.

Fortunately, I am married to an accountant—you can't get much more detail-oriented than that. When we first met, my wife Kay was a call centre consultant. Her role in sales and marketing was preceded by a long career at the post office. In a variety of admin roles she held in her late teens and early twenties, she exhibited early signs of her attention-to-detail prowess. In fact, if they were handing out gold medals for attention to detail, Kay would be at the head of the line to receive hers!

In 2005, Kay and I found ourselves in the market for a new home. I knew what I was looking for. I could visualise the look and feel of the house, the number of bedrooms, the maturity of the garden, etc. The trouble was that I couldn't get Kay to 'see' the same things as me.

With pen and paper in hand, she sat me down and started to write out a list of what we were looking for: four bedrooms, a study, a separate dining area from the kitchen, a family room, the size of the land we were buying. The list kept growing....

Soon we were listing the suburb we wanted to live in and the proximity to motorways, schools, and shopping malls. Not a single detail was left out. By the time we counted them all up, the requirements totalled twenty-two. Then Kay and I added the twenty-third item to the list—the price we were willing to pay for the property.

Armed with the list in our hands, we started to visit real estate agents in our desired suburbs. They were all impressed with the thoughtful detail we provided them. I suspect we represented a very small minority of their clientele. Unfortunately, most of them either burst into laughter or simply shook their heads when they concluded our list.

"You'll never find a house for *that* price in this suburb!" they would chuckle.

Needless to say, *they* didn't receive any commission cheques from us.

Having such an extensive list made the search easier—we could exclude certain properties without having to see them, which saved a lot of time! As time was running out for us and we had to get out of the house we had sold, we weren't tempted to buy the wrong house just to have somewhere to go—the list helped us to avoid a costly mistake.

As a leader, you still need to have some attention to detail. The most logical starting point is to begin writing out your lists. They serve a number of useful purposes:

- They capture your thoughts on paper.
- They give you a fall-back position that stops things from 'slipping your mind'.
- They help you clarify your thoughts.
- They enable you to prioritise your requirements.
- They trigger the reticular activator in your brain.
- They help you to attract your heart's desire towards you.

What is your current thinking when it comes to making lists? Are you a dedicated scribbler, or do you tend to rely on your memory? When has creating a list led to a positive outcome for you?

I encourage you to start making lists as one of your good daily habits.

Oh, in case you were wondering, yes, we did find a house that met *all* of our documented requirements. Go on, give it a go; write your list, and see what happens!

LIST OF THINGS I WANT IN LIFE

Are You Behind Before You Ever Get Started?

At times, you might feel as if the whole world is conspiring to get you. No matter what you want to accomplish, your 'To-Do' list seems to be sitting around the 1,002 mark, and nothing you can do will make you see the light at the end of the tunnel.

If you can relate to this, then let me introduce you to Marla Cilley—also known as the FlyLady. Since 1999, she has been a mentor to over half-a-million people, teaching them how to organize their homes and how to love themselves. (You can find out more about her at FlyLady.net.)

I first heard about the FlyLady a number of years ago, and that was when I was introduced to my first Flying lesson—Shiny Sink 101. Picture the scene. A solo-parent has three young children, all under the age of five, while trying to keep control over her household. No matter what she does, she can never seem to get ahead.

One day, tired from chasing after her children, she is dead beat and ready to crawl into bed. As she walks past her kitchen, she sees the all-too-familiar sight of a sink full of dirty dishes. For a split second, something snaps in her mind. Enough is enough!

Despite her draining energy levels, she pushes through and makes a concerted effort to clean the dishes, and she goes to bed with a clean and shiny sink. The following morning, the sound of her children abruptly wakes her and that gut-wrenching feeling of having to start all over again takes grip. But this day is different from the previous ones.

When she enters the kitchen, she remembers she had cleaned the sink. What greets her is a sparkling sink. For the first time in a long time, she is not starting behind the eight-ball! The sight lifts her spirit.

Thus begins a daily habit. Every night, just before she goes to bed, she makes sure she cleans the sink. The task takes no more than fifteen minutes, and despite her tiredness, the reward of waking up to a clean scene is enough to keep her going.

Soon she extends the same principle to other rooms in her house. She will allocate a fifteen-minute period to start tackling each task. Armed with some cleaning utensils and a stop clock, she goes to work and does as much as fifteen minutes will allow.

The results, whilst not instantaneous, help her to develop the habits that improve her surroundings and lift her self-esteem.

Take a look at your surroundings and ask yourself, "What can I do to make it more attractive?"

Apply the FlyLady principle and tackle the task ahead with gusto. Limit yourself to fifteen minutes, and make sure you stop whatever you are doing to step back and admire the progress you have made. Then, if time permits, give yourself another fifteen-minute window and do a bit more. You'll be surprised how quickly you will make a difference in your surroundings.

Are You Taught to Be Complex or Is It Simply Effective?

What the FlyLady recommends is simple enough. Yet simplicity is often thrown away for a more complex solution. I love a quote from Warren Buffett: "The business schools reward difficult, complex behaviour more than simple behaviour, but simple behaviour is more effective."

Why do we tend to overcomplicate things?

When I set up my network marketing business in the late 1990s, I was affiliated with the Amway Corporation and a support system developed by an organisation named Network 21. The best way to describe the synergy between these two entities is to think about how you bake a cake—Amway provided the ingredients, and Network 21 provided the recipe.

Network 21 was the brainchild of Jim and Nancy Dornan, who had built a successful multi-million business and had understood the pitfalls and strategies required to succeed. They had put together a 'paint by numbers' system to support IBO's (Independent Business Owners) like myself and my wife as we ventured into our own business.

Yet, despite their obvious experience and authority in this domain, I took it upon myself to 'improve' their system by creating Network 22, Network 23, and Network 24. Unfortunately, none of my modifications were duplicable, nor did they enhance my business growth.

Why do we feel we have to tinker with things to change the simple—yet effective—into the complex and destructive? I believe the answer lies in Warren's quote...our education systems reward the difficult and complex behaviours over the simple and effective!

I encourage you as a leader to consider the following five concepts when you are looking at changing an existing system.

1. If it ain't broke—don't fix it. As long as a system or process you are using works, keep utilising it as long as it

doesn't cost you money or lose you customers.

2. Just because it is simple, it doesn't mean you have to make it complex. Sometimes, simple is better.
3. Seek counsel from experienced individuals. Go to someone with a track record and ask for his or her opinion.
4. If you seek counsel, listen to it. Don't ask someone for an opinion and then ignore it.
5. Ask yourself, "What can I simplify in my life?" If your life is overly-complicated right now, something has to give.

As you carry on with your day today, make sure you use the 'K.I.S.S.' principle: Keep It Short and Simple!

Applying lessons from Nelson Mandela's life:

Key #14 - DEVELOPING GOOD DAILY HABITS

Mandela understood the hardships of prison, so he started to train his body to live on less even before he was sentenced. That meant that he was berated for being too thin. (It was an African custom to acknowledge wealth and success through a fuller figure.)

In prison, exercise became a routine that helped Mandela in many different ways. Initially, the prisoners received their exercise through hard manual labour. But even that, over time, they successfully managed to petition to be removed.

An unanticipated result of ending manual labour was that Mandela started to gain weight. The daily walk to the quarry helped to keep him trim, but now exercise took on even more importance, not only for his physical health, but also for his peace of mind. He found that exercise helped him to dissipate tension, which was the enemy of serenity. Mandela wrote:

"Many times in the old days I unleashed my anger and frustrations on a punching bag rather than taking it out on a comrade or even a policeman.... I found that I worked better and thought more clearly when I was in good physical condition."

Leaders have to have the mental strength to think things through in a clear and concise fashion ahead of having physical strength. Mandela demonstrated the benefits of keeping his mind sharp to enable him to lead with clarity. And you will need a clear head to navigate the course ahead....

"In prison, having an outlet for my frustrations was absolutely essential."

— Nelson Mandela

Key #15

PLANNING AHEAD IS KEY

"A goal without a plan is just a wish."

— Antoine de Saint-Exupéry

Developing daily habits becomes more critical as you grow in your leadership. The bigger the scale, the less you can rely on your memory. Systems have to be put into place and better disciplines have to become ingrained in your psyche. When you are leading an organisation into a long-term project, your ability to plan ahead is critical to your success. There is an ancient Jewish proverb that asks, "Would you venture into battle if you did not have the funds to pay for your army?" This key will help you understand the importance of future-proofing and succession planning.

How Can You Make More?

If I were to ask you, "How can I make more money?" I wonder what response I would get.

They say that which you pursue will elude you like the butterfly you try to catch in the garden. No matter how hard you try, you'll fail. But if you stand still, the butterfly will often come to you... and settle on your shoulder.

Recently, one of my mentors—Scott Fay—shared a great teaching lesson derived from a quote by Jim Rohn that states, "If you want to do, be or have more, you have to become more."

Who would you become?

It all boils down to one core philosophy—if you want to earn more, give more!

Instead of focusing on the number you'd like to get (e.g., $100K or $250K), focus on what you want to *give*.

John Maxwell encourages people to become a river and not a reservoir. Allow things to flow through you—*not* just to you. In order for you to add value to others, you need to share with them the wisdom you have gathered.

There are five things I encourage you to become:

1. **More Aware:** It's not motivating enough to think, "I'm going to give more away!" I encourage you to become more aware of the needs that are out there. Ask yourself, "*Who* will I give it away to?" and "*Why* will I give it away?" If you can attach it to the need, the concept of giving becomes easier. Being aware of the need helps you to attach to the need.

2. **More Convicted:** Passion is when you get excited about something. But when you get convicted, that becomes the great motivator that helps you put your passion to work. It turns your idea into a reality. And that's where you can make a difference!

3. **More Productive:** Don't play the 'should' game. Should I do this or should I do that? What is easy to do is just as

easy not to do. People living in a hurricane-prone region get very productive 24-48 hours before the hurricane hits. They become focused because they have a *why*.

4. **More Generous:** If you don't learn to give when you have a little, you'll never learn to give when you have a lot. Be generous with your time and your resources. Don't limit yourself to making donations to charities; contribute your time to good causes—like helping widows, 'big buddy' an orphaned child, or mentor a new business. If, like me, you are a person of faith, you may want to give your tithe to your church. Give it out of a generous heart—not out of a religious viewpoint. And as you increase your tithe over time, see your income grow accordingly!
5. **More Significant:** I want to encourage you to become more significant as you make a bigger impact on the world that surrounds you. By being a river and not a reservoir, you can move from success to significance by thinking about others and giving more to help them.

As a leader, I want you to review your business and set the vision and goals for the business year ahead. I encourage you to become these five things, which will help you to start planning ahead and to see the financial benefits flow into your business as a result.

WHAT NEED CAN I ATTACH MYSELF TO AND WHY?

What Are You Asking For?

When I was hired by SITEL as the product development manager, I was tasked to undertake a benchmarking survey for the directory assistance industry. The challenge was that this would be the first survey of its kind, so I had no idea whom to include in it, and it was to be an international survey. Oh, and did I mention that I had never run a benchmarking survey before?

No problem—I'm a Kiwi, and we're accustomed to using #8 wire to fix things. (In case you were wondering what #8 wire is, it's our version of 'duct tape'—it'll fix anything!)

Armed with a whiteboard and a marker pen, I scratched my head and started to write down what I needed. I set the goal for the number of participants in the survey—seven, including ourselves. I identified the ideal geographies: North America, Canada, Asia, Australasia.

Then I worked on the list of organisations I knew. In North America, the major Telcos were the easiest to identify: AT&T, Verizon, Bell South, and Bell Canada. In Australia, it was Telstra. That was a starting point.

And that was where I drew a blank. How was I going to get close to them? I had very few contacts I could directly approach, so I went back through all of my colleagues within Telecom New Zealand and started to list their names to touch base with them for any contacts they might have. After all, it's not what you know, but who you know that makes a difference (see Key #11 for the first lesson in life I learned from my dad).

Then I took a step back, looked at my list, and thought for a while, before returning and writing the following: "Anybody who can lead me to the right people!"

With that task completed, I shut down my laptop and packed up my bag to go home.

I'm a firm believer in writing down my goals. As I describe in Key #14—Developing Daily Habits, something called the reticular activator kicks in inside your brain when you write things down. It's almost as if the Grand Overall Designer conspires to bring the things you are asking for directly to you.

Within a couple of days, I received a printed newsletter that was forwarded to me from our client. He thought it might be of use. It included information about one of the leading database providers for the directory assistance industry—a company called LSSi. To be honest, none of us had ever heard of this company. It was based in New York and had a generic email listed for its sales division.

I decided to send LSSi an introductory email to ask whether anyone there could help me identify the right individuals and organisations that would like to participate in the first global benchmarking survey for directory assistance. I explained who I was and what my role was. I went on to tell them that our company outsourced all of Telecom New Zealand's calls. And I finished off the email with the magic nine-word phrase I had learned in Bob Burg's book *Winning Without Intimidation*: "If you can't help me, then I'll definitely understand!"

Nothing ventured, nothing gained.

The following morning, I received an email from a lovely man by the name of Harry Petit, who was a Founder of LSSi. He told me my email had been forwarded to him and he was willing to help me. Petit gave me his direct dial number in the U.S., and he encouraged me to call him. Bingo!

Petit was the best thing since sliced bread. Not only did he have all the contacts within the Telcos that I was targeting, but he even opened up new avenues with the likes of Cincinnati Bell and others in the Philippines.

How often do you write down your goals? Are they in front of you on a daily basis, or just written down and consigned to a dusty, shadowy folder in your filing cabinet?

Take the time to write down your top five goals for the short term (next twelve months), medium term (next five years), and long term (ten-plus years) in the space below. Once you've written them, prioritise them from the most important to the least.

GOALS	
SHORT-TERM (NEXT 12 MONTHS)	**PRIORITY**
1.	
2.	
3.	
4.	
5.	
MEDIUM-TERM (NEXT 5 YEARS)	**PRIORITY**
1.	
2.	
3.	
4.	
5.	
LONG-TERM (NEXT 10+ YEARS)	**PRIORITY**
1.	
2.	
3.	
4.	
5.	

Are You Using the Power of Pictures?

Having experienced success with written goals, I decided to expand this technique to include visual images. Ever since I had lived in the UK, I'd had a fascination with the auto manufacturer SAAB. This Swedish company had created a memorable advertising campaign that had a lasting effect on me.

I started out by finding a screen saver from SAAB to adorn my laptop. It kicked in if my laptop was idle for five minutes or more. I swear I started seeing this screensaver in my dreams.

After a while, I was bold enough to take a SAAB out for a test drive. When I got it home, I parked it in my driveway and got Kay to take pictures of me standing beside the car and even seated behind the wheel. I used these pictures to create a collage that I kept on my desk at work, in the inside of my compendium, and on the dashboard of my car.

I had been introduced to this technique during my Amway days. We were encouraged to create a dream board—a visual representation of the dreams and goals we wanted to achieve in life. Often it's less about stuff we want than it is about whom we want to be in this world.

In my case, the dream to own a SAAB materialised within twelve months of creating that dream board. I ended up owning a SAAB 9-3 Aero, which at full list price was worth $84,000. It was an ex-demonstrator, with 20,000 kms on the clock, but ended up being an absolute bargain for around 40 percent of the retail value. But that's another story for another time!

Are You Asking the Right Questions to Improve Your Planning?

We can probably agree that writing down your goals is important, and visualising them through dream boards can be very powerful. But don't forget to ask the right questions as you plan ahead.

During the last year of my bachelor's degree in the UK, I spent a lot of time cramming and studying with my fellow students.

We would invest hours on end to going through the mock questions and regurgitating the equations and formulas that had framed our education.

One topic, however, we kept stumbling on as we studied late into the night. After a couple of failed attempts to get the answer right, we decided it was time for us to seek professional advice.

At the next opportunity, we went to the lecture halls and waited outside our tutor's office in the hope that we could catch him between lectures. Luck was on our side since he happened to be free. We were ushered into his office, and he sat us down opposite him at his desk.

"How can I help you lads?" he asked.

We explained that one aspect of the lecture notes had us baffled and we needed to understand the concept behind the question.

"Why do you want to know that?" he asked.

Because we wanted to learn how to answer the question. Duh. Why was he asking that question!

"But how will it help you?" he continued with his line of questioning.

Honestly, by now we were getting frustrated. We wanted to learn, but he was refusing to teach us. We could not understand what was causing the impasse.

"Learning about this topic will not help you in the exam," he went on to say. "If I were you, I would focus on other topics...."

It took us a while to understand where his questions were leading us. But finally, the penny dropped... the topic we were desperate to learn about wasn't even featured in the final exam!

And that was when I learned the importance of not only planning ahead (studying for our exams), but asking the questions that help you make wise choices in determining what to focus on.

Can You Be Larger than Life?

As a sales representative in the UK, I worked for a small I.T. company based in Blackburn, Lancashire. We were a start-up organisation with only eight employees, yet our aspirations were much larger than the eight of us.

My fondest recollection of that time was a story that was shared about an audacious marketing campaign. During the company's infancy, when it had only three employees, it was targeting a specific account, but it was unsuccessful in moving beyond the preliminary meetings. The employees knew who the key decision maker was in the company, but he just wasn't interested in taking things any further.

During a meeting with the key decision maker, our sales director noticed a billboard almost directly opposite his office window. In casual conversation, he also learned that his prospect travelled the same route to and from work each day. Further investigation of that route revealed another billboard along the route. Soon a plan was hatched and a marketing campaign was birthed.

Once those two billboards were rented, our company stood front and centre in the prospect's life.

As he drove in to work, he would pass our billboard. As he sat in his office, he would stare out at our billboard. As he journeyed home, guess what...he drove right past our billboard.

Within a few months, he was more receptive to our advances, and he eventually purchased from us. After signing the contract, he found out we had only three employees at that time in the UK. He was surprised. His impression was that we were a much larger organisation. You will be surprised what a large 'dream board' can do for you!

Applying lessons from Nelson Mandela's life:

Key #15 - PLANNING AHEAD IS KEY

From time to time, while Mandela was in prison, the warders would try to engage the prisoners in conversation. One particular warder, a young man who arrived in 1969, seemed particularly eager to develop a relationship with Mandela. Over time, this warder let Mandela know he was planning his escape.

The warder's plan was first to drug the warders on duty at the lighthouse. Then he would supply Mandela with a key to get out of his section. Mandela would then meet a boat, equipped with underwater diving gear, that would land on the beach.

Mandela would then use the underwater gear to swim into the harbour at Cape Town, where he would be collected and taken to a local airport to be flown out of the country.

Having listened to the farfetched plan in its entirety, Mandela consulted with Walter Sisulu, one of the founding members of the High Organ: "[W]e agreed that this fellow was not to be trusted. I never told him that I would not do it, but I never took any of the actions required to implement the plan."

The warder, it turned out, was an agent of the Bureau of State Security (BOSS), South Africa's secret intelligence agency. It wasn't long before he was transferred off the island.

A good leader doesn't move impulsively into action without exploring the full picture and thinking three or four steps into the future. By planning ahead, Mandela was able to ensure that the pathway chosen was safe to travel on....

"Whenever a new commanding officer was appointed, I requested a meeting with him. I did this in order to impress upon him the seriousness of our cause and also to evaluate his character."

— Nelson Mandela

Key #16

ENCOURAGING YOUR PEOPLE IS IMPORTANT

"You cannot expect victory and plan for defeat."

— Joel Osteen

Once you have started to plan ahead, make sure you include regular encouragement for your team. A strong leader will not only be a great vision caster, but he or she will also be an incredible encourager. There will be times when you will need your team members to go the extra mile and do things they don't necessarily want to do. When implemented, this key can produce an extra 10 percent from individuals who already seem to be giving their all.

How Are You Casting Your Vision?

I love watching leaders and learning as much as I can from them. In 2005, I was encouraged to attend an evening service at a church that my good friends and business mentors, Simon and Yvonne Godfrey, attended.

City Impact Church is a nondenominational church of faith with Pentecostal beliefs based in East Coast Bays, New Zealand. Formerly known as Bays Christian Fellowship, it was founded in 1982 by current senior pastors and husband and wife Peter and Bev Mortlock. This vibrant church attracts people of all ages, across multiple cultural groups and socio-demographic sectors. But one common theme holds them all together: Peter Mortlock.

Peter Mortlock is a testament to Key #1 in leadership: 'Everything rises and falls on leadership.' I have been a member of his congregation since January 2005, and over the years, I have seen him cast a vision and inspire his congregation to go to amazing heights.

In his book *Grateful: 30 Years of City Impact Church*, Mortlock shares his journey of how he planted the church and gave his first sermon. He says, "I have to confess, I did not feel ready to do this, and I remember sharing this with Bev's Mum, who gave me some sound advice. 'Peter,' she said, 'If you wait till you think you are ready—you never will be!'"

If you are waiting for the 'right time', you could be waiting a long time. A leader will need to take action before waiting for the motivation to kick in. You could be waiting for the planets to align or the perfect storm to arrive. That may never happen.

Mortlock is a great visionary. He can encourage his congregation to accomplish things most pastors would never consider. In 2005, he was approached by Syd Jones, an elder in the church, with plans to build a 2,200-seat auditorium. Jones believed it could be built by the congregation—a task never previously accomplished in New Zealand.

It took the vision casting of a true leader to encourage the congregation to give up its Saturday mornings for eighteen months. And how did Mortlock do it? Simply by implementing the following seven steps:

1. **He created a 3-D model of the building.** This model enabled the congregation to see the final product before it was even built.
2. **He led from the front.** He was visible on site every week, and he made sure he greeted everyone there.
3. **He gave regular (weekly) updates:** Each Sunday morning, he would play a video of what had been accomplished the day before, with a call for more to join the following week.
4. **He gave everyone a role:** If you could bake, you were encouraged to feed the troops. (They say the way to a man's heart is through his stomach!)
5. **He made it look fun:** Each weekly video update included scenes of people laughing and enjoying themselves.
6. **He made sacrifices:** He gave up every Saturday for eighteen months.
7. **He worked to his strength:** Although he was capable of doing any number of tasks, he chose to collect the rubbish around the site each week because it gave him the opportunity to be seen by and to interact with every volunteer.

The next time you have a big project that requires buy-in from your team, consider how you can use this seven-step model to your advantage to encourage your team to go the extra mile.

Do You Know What Salmon Is?

In the mid-1980s, I was employed by a company headquartered

in Portland, Oregon in the United States. A colleague and I travelled there from the UK for four weeks on a project. We were both in our mid-twenties and life was one big adventure to us then.

The company put us up in a self-contained apartment that catered to all our needs. We were given $500 in cash to take care of any out-of-pocket expenses, which to us, at the time, represented a lot of money!

Our journey started out in style. The plane was almost completely empty, and it felt as if there were more crew on board than passengers! At LAX, we transitioned from one terminal to another as we caught our connecting flight and used the remainder of the weekend to acclimatise.

At the time, the company, which was headquartered in Beaverton, employed more than 24,000 people. On Monday, when we entered their offices for the first time, the news headlines broadcast a gloomy picture. Fifteen thousand employees were being laid off!

As you can imagine, the work atmosphere was very low-spirited. Many were uncertain about their long-term futures.

And you guessed it—two young men with heavy British accents stood out a mile from the rest of the crowd.

Despite the difficult situation, we tried our best to hunker down and get involved in our project. Meetings were held with our counterparts and we continued to press forward. Resistance was encountered the majority of the time. People were cautious of our intentions. It was easy to feel disheartened with the situation, except for the one bright spot....

Marcy was a solo-mum and the sweetest person anybody could meet. Like a mother hen, she took us under her wing and very quickly developed a strong relationship with us. She made sure we knew our way around, made introductions to the senior executives who could positively influence the outcome of our work, and pointed us to shopping malls and supermarkets where we could supply our needs at affordable prices.

One day, Marcy invited us over for dinner at her home. She opened up the conversation with the following question. "Have you ever eaten salmon before? It's a special kind of fish."

For the foodies amongst us, salmon is often referred to as the 'king of fish'. It was not the most common fish in the UK, so it had a reputation as one of the most expensive. Yet here was a solo-mum, bringing up a teenage daughter on what we suspected was near minimum wage, spending her hard-earned income to feed two guests.

I don't know about you, but if I were unsure where my next paycheque was coming from, I might have thought twice about spending it on two strangers!

Yet Marcy's simple gesture had profound meaning. She demonstrated a fundamental trait of leadership that belied her position within the company. She used the key principle that "Encouraging Your People Is Important."

WHOM DO I NEED TO ENCOURAGE?	WHY DO I NEED TO ENCOURAGE THEM?

Are You Confident Enough to Turn the Chair?

It is easy to get discouraged. You just have to watch some of the reality TV programs where contestants audition in front of audiences or judges with the intention of finding their fame and fortune. There is one in particular I have been watching, *The Voice Kids (Australia)*, and I have been blown away!

If you haven't watched *The Voice*, let me quickly share the show's format. Young kids get up on stage and audition by singing to a group of judges. The twist is that the judges cannot see them perform because they are sitting in chairs with their backs to the singers.

All they can hear is the voice of the person auditioning!

The judges then have to decide whether they want to coach these kids—who are as young as eight years old! What a hard task. How would you cope with the pressure?

As I started to think through this situation, as the President of the National Speakers Association of New Zealand, I wondered what lessons we, as leaders, could learn to apply within our businesses. Like the children, we are projecting our 'voices' to attract a clientele that (in some cases) hasn't even seen us.

The biggest challenge is that, like the kids on *The Voice*, we risk being rejected by the judges. And their opinion of us can affect our self-esteem.

So the question I would ask you to ponder is, "How are you using your 'voice' to convince your clients to press their red buttons and turn their chairs to select you as their next client...?" What are you doing out there to hone your craft? Here are five suggestions for you to consider:

1. **Are you picking up the phone and speaking to each and**

every organisation that is willing to listen? You don't have to say too much; just ask for some time to have a quick cup of coffee.

2. **Do you have mentors you can go to for advice?** I call it an 'inner circle'. This handful of people is selected to help you expand your business by surrounding you with the skill-sets you lack.
3. **Are you recording your presentations and workshops?** Taking time to go back and review your work is very powerful. If you are not booking P.W.S. (Personal White Space) into your calendar, then you are letting yourself down. Take the time to be alone—no cellphone, emails, or music; no interruptions—and use it to review your progress to date. You'll be surprised what you discover!
4. **Have you received client testimonials, and are they on your website?** Have you gone back to your clients and asked them for their positive feedback? If they give it to you, ask them for a helping hand...ask them for a referral. Chances are quite strong that they will oblige!
5. **Are you investing in your personal growth?** As I've said before, you are either 'green and growing or ripe and rotting'! Whatever you put into yourself will eventually have to come back out. If you are not investing in a personal growth course or—even better still—in a personal coach, take stock of where you are at and make the decision to 'turn your chair' and back yourself!

As you contemplate these five points, I wish you all the best. May the desires of your heart be matched by the turning chairs of the judges!

Applying lessons from Nelson Mandela's life:

Key #16 - ENCOURAGING YOUR PEOPLE IS IMPORTANT

Whilst at Robben Island, Mandela knew the warder who was in charge of the prisoners at the quarry. Known as 'Zithulele', the Quiet One, he was a tolerant and soft-spoken individual. He was more concerned with orderly behaviour than specific outcomes of the work the prisoners did. Rarely did he berate them when they were discovered leaning on their spades, talking. And often, he would maintain a large distance from them when they were working.

One day in 1966, this warder approached the prisoners with a request for help. Mandela writes: "[H]e came to us and said, 'Gentlemen, the rains have washed away the lines on the roads; we need twenty kilos of lime today. Can you help?' Although we were working very little at the time, he had approached us as human beings, and we agreed to assist him."

The simple act of acknowledging that the prisoners under his command were human beings went a long way towards gaining cooperation from a group of people who would normally not be inclined to help. By applying this leadership key, the warder encouraged people to join him on his journey....

"When the water starts boiling it is foolish to turn off the heat."

— Nelson Mandela

Key #17

REWARDING GOOD BEHAVIOUR HAS TO HAPPEN REGULARLY

"Act the way you'd like to be and soon you'll be the way you act."

— George W. Crane

I would be really pleased to hear you say that you already encourage your team—that handwritten notes wing their way around the office and you live in a high-tech world that is supplemented with a high-touch. But be careful that this isn't a short-term fad. Ensure that it becomes ingrained into the fabric of your organisation's culture. Implementing this key on a regular basis will enhance your position as a leader. It will lead to loyalty.

Is Your Loyalty Being Rewarded?

Back in 2000, I was travelling extensively to the U.S. and Europe as part of my work. I had accumulated so many airpoints that I soon found myself in a meteoric rise as far as my status went with our local carrier—Air New Zealand. Before I knew it, I had reached its top tier status, Gold Elite.

That opened doors for me, and the service I experienced was second to none. It was during a heady time when you could accumulate airpoints and redeem them for long-haul flights. Soon I was returning to the UK, and I had enough airpoints to qualify for an upgrade into business class for myself, my wife, and our seven-month-old daughter.

With a change of roles, my travel schedule declined as did my status with the airline.

Over the last five years, I started to increase my international travel, and for many years, I managed to improve my status slightly from the baseline—jade—through to the next tier—silver—oscillating between the two. The benefits were commensurate with the status, and the best reward I managed to get was two complimentary visits to the Koru Lounge when I was flying.

I did have an option to purchase Koru Club membership, but that was in the region of $750 per year, and I never saw the immediate value in making such an investment.

Then I decided to invest more in my education and networking, and I started to attend more international conventions. Soon, I found myself flying to Singapore, Australia, the United States, the United Kingdom, and even Malaysia.

At first, I would select the cheapest airline ticket to get to my destination. Often, that meant a longer layover, or an additional leg, and invariably, it would route via Australia and through a different carrier. Whilst the savings were significant, the improvement in status with any of the carriers was non-existent.

Quickly, I realised that if I stuck with one carrier, I would receive loyalty benefits.

I soon decided I would use Air New Zealand as my primary carrier, and if I couldn't, I would ask the travel agent to route me via a Star Alliance partner so I could accumulate the status points. This strategy provided immediate results, and soon my status climbed back up to silver and then to gold. And with gold, I had complimentary access to the Koru Lounge for a year.

If you have to travel a lot, and you find yourself in an international airport, you will probably relate to the challenges of sitting at the departure gate waiting for your boarding call. The seats are rigid, the space is cramped, and there are few amenities. The Koru Lounge, on the other hand, is opulent. Food and drink overflows, free WiFi is abundant, and the service is second to none.

When I post on Facebook that I'm about to depart and I tag myself at the Koru Lounge at an international terminal, people comment on how 'lucky' I am. Luck, my friend, has nothing to do with it. I'm simply a devoted client who is being rewarded for loyal and good behaviour!

Are You Doing Good Things to Others?

We have all heard the phrase, "Do unto others as you would like done unto you." Some think of it as 'karma'. What goes around, comes around.

As a leader, you need to recognise the good in the people who surround you. Everybody is looking for some form of recognition, and as a leader, you have to jump on any sign of good behaviour and reward it. And the key is in the speed of acknowledgement.

A number of years ago, I worked hard on a project at work. It involved late nights and coordination of internal and external suppliers. We were under a deadline to deliver, and we knew there was a compliance element to it. If we got that wrong, we would be eliminated from a short-list on a multi-million dollar opportunity.

You may recall me referencing earlier that 39 percent of employees feel underappreciated at work, whilst 77 percent of employees stated they would work harder if given more recognition!

After the hard work and the long nights I put into the response, I headed overseas for a short break with my wife. At the airport, waiting for our boarding call, I received a phone call from my boss. He informed me I was receiving a commendation for all my hard work. I must admit I was pretty pleased. It was the first one I had received within that role.

I had no idea what the reward would be, but I looked forward to receiving it the following week when I returned to work.

However, when I returned, a few days turned into a week and then a month. Whatever the reward was, nobody within my team seemed to know what it was or who had it. Was it a financial reward? A gift voucher? A bottle of wine? Whatever it was, my euphoria over being recognised was tarnished by the lack of the prize. The good intentions of that reward were lost on me. It never came, and to this day, I have no idea what I missed out on. For all intentions, it felt as if they had thrown me aside like an unwanted Christmas present.

In your role as a leader, how do you respond to good behaviour? Do you just take it for granted, or do you make a song and dance over it? Are you seizing the moment, or letting it slip through your fingers? Good work requires instant recognition.

WAYS TO REWARD GOOD BEHAVIOUR

Are You Punishing Poor Behaviour?

The flip side of the coin is poor behaviour. What is your policy for addressing poor behaviour?

When I was party president for the Family Party, we instituted a policy that press releases would come through either our leader, Richie Lewis, or myself. It was important that members of the press could identify the key players they could approach for comment and that we were timely and consistent in our communication.

One day, after the election, I woke up to see a press release on one of our online newsfeeds. It was unauthorised, and it pointed to internal conflict within the party. To say I was less than impressed would be an understatement!

When you release something to the media, your email address gets attached to the press release. Therefore, it becomes very easy to track down the leak within your organisation. There, in electronic black and white, was the name and email of one of our candidates. It was the equivalent of a digital fingerprint that identified the perpetrator!

To address this issue, we knew we had to act swiftly. I made immediate contact with our leadership team and we arranged for a meeting with our candidate. I called the candidate up and asked for an immediate explanation on the phone about the press release. Incredibly, the candidate denied involvement. The next step was a meeting in person, which I facilitated.

We needed to implement immediate action. And the guilty party needed to understand the consequences of his action and receive a punishment commensurate with his misconduct.

If an issue occurs within your team, what measures are you willing to take to address them? What is the process you will follow?

I recommend you take the following seven steps:

1. Contact your leadership team
2. Document the issue
3. Connect with the offender
4. Arrange to have a second support person from your team be with you in person when meeting with the offender
5. Document the meeting and hand out minutes
6. Do all of the above within twenty-four hours of the issue coming to the surface
7. Follow up with the guilty party within a week to ensure that agreed actions are implemented

Applying lessons from Nelson Mandela's life:

Key #17 - REWARDING GOOD BEHAVIOUR HAS TO HAPPEN REGULARLY

In Key #4, we explored the way the prisoners were classified. They entered the prison as a D classification, which held the least privileges possible. Over time, through good behaviour and 'towing the line', each prisoner could improve his classification status to reach an A classification.

These measures were put in place not only to reward good behaviour, but also to stop unwanted conduct. Unfortunately, it was viewed as a demeaning and corrupt practice. It was used to repress prisoners in general and political prisoners in particular. "We despised the classification system," Mandela comments.

The reward system can be used to good effect by great leaders. Whilst temptation exists to create a system that can be used as a carrot to reward the good undertaken by others, you have to make sure it is not used predominantly as a stick to punish people for petty misdemeanours.

Ensure that you have enough rewards in place to be accessible at all levels. Sometimes, the fact that the right behaviour is recognised and rewarded in a timely fashion—even if it is done verbally—has more power than the size of the reward.

As a leader, make sure you are always on the lookout for good behaviour and ensure that you can reward it instantaneously. By implementing rewards for good behaviour, you can make the path more comfortable for fellow travellers hiking alongside you....

"As a D group prisoner, I was entitled to have only one visitor, and write and receive only one letter every six months. I found this one of the most inhumane restrictions of the prison system. Communication with one's family is a human right; it should not be restricted by the artificial gradations of a prison system. But it was one of the facts of prison life."

— Nelson Mandela

Key #18

GIVING IT OVER TO GOD

"Now to Him who is able to do exceedingly abundantly above all that we ask or think, according to the power that works in us...."

— Ephesians 3:20

Whether or not you believe in a Higher Being, I think you will agree with me that doing it all by yourself can be draining. What if you can hook into something that is bigger that yourself? In this key, I will help you explore the opportunities of wisdom that my faith has revealed to me. It is through this key that I have liberated my greatest leadership potential. By releasing my grip on it, I was able to accomplish more.

Are You Trying to Do It All By Yourself?

I promised you earlier in this book that I would give you ample warning when I am ready to share about my faith. Consider yourself warned! This is your chance to turn the page, or even skip this key. But I would not be true to my faith and my Grand

Overall Designer (G.O.D.) if I were to omit this section.

I grew up in a Christian household. My father was born in Jerusalem and my mother in Bethlehem. You couldn't get any closer to the biblical epicentre! Both my parents were Greek Orthodox Christians, which meant they were quite religious. I have found that when it comes to God, you can either be religious or create a relationship. I would encourage you to foster the latter.

Let me qualify what I mean by 'religious'. The Greek Orthodox Church can seem quite prescriptive in the way its Church is run. It has multiple icons in its churches, which you are expected to kiss and pray in front of. Incense is burned at every given opportunity, and it is accompanied with a lot of prayers that can sound like chanting to people outside of the Church. Whilst the purpose is to pray to the saints who are represented by the icons, it can be misconstrued as an idolatry.

For a long time, I accompanied my parents to church. The services were delivered in Greek (I could swear it was Ancient Greek!), and none of the liturgy made any sense to me. I was told when to stand up and when to sit down. When to bow my head and when to perform the 'Sign of the Cross'. This routine was easy to follow, but it did nothing for my spiritual fulfillment or my personal wellbeing.

I was still the dunce in my class. I was still sabotaging my career and my relationships.

Which Question Would You Answer?

When I was eleven, I started attending boarding school in the UK. When I visited the housemaster, he sat me down in the armchair opposite his. All the boys went through this ritual, so I had been coached by my peers.

As the youngest boy in the year, I was the last to go through this ceremony. My housemaster would clear his throat and start the conversation by stating that he was about to ask me two questions. The first I was expected to answer, but the second did not require an obligatory answer.

The first question was, “Where do babies come from?” I guess that was my sex education taken care of!

The second question was, “Do you believe in God?” To be honest, since I was a believer at the time, I thought the second question was a lot easier to answer than the first!

My personal journey with God started at an early age. I remember attending Sunday school classes when I was growing up in Libya and getting so excited to hear the different stories from the Old and New Testaments. By the time we lived in London, I had joined a Christian youth organisation called the Crusaders.

The organisation’s vision was to proclaim the Gospel of Jesus Christ to students in the UK, to nurture Christians, to encourage church membership, and to train young Christians for a life of servant leadership. For a young man, I was quite invigorated by the organisation’s energy of the leadership and its catchy hymns accompanied by acoustic guitars. The gospels came alive whenever I attended one of the meetings.

I knew God had sent down His only beloved Son to earth so He could die for our sins on a cross. My relationship with Jesus was as real as if I were having a relationship with you. In my mind, there was no doubt that God was real.

But when I was fifteen years old, I came unstuck and my faith was derailed. All because I fell into a religious loophole. During a Bible study group, the eldest boy finished the session by suggesting we close in prayer. He raised his hands and head towards heaven and started to pray.

The Greek Orthodox Church taught us to be pious and bow our heads in submission to God, so when I saw him looking toward heaven, my religious instincts kicked in, and I immediately accused the boy of being a Pharisee. I told him he was a clean cup on the outside, but dirty on the inside.

The result of this outburst was that I ended up being caned by my housemaster for refusing to apologise to the other boy. Then I felt I had been let down by God. He never intervened to stop the caning. Hurt and disappointed, I simply walked away from Him.

It would be nearly thirty years before I realigned my relationship with Him.

What Is Your #1 Short-Term Priority?

Towards the end of 2004, my wife Kay and I were invited to a business counselling meeting with our up-line diamonds, Simon and Yvonne Godfrey. They combined the event with dinner since it was around the time of our wedding anniversary.

We were tasked to write down our goals in three categories—for the short-term (twelve months), medium term (five years), and long term (ten-plus years). In addition, we were asked to prioritise them from the most important to the least. After dinner, I offered to go first in sharing my lists.

At the top of my short-term goal list was to be planted in a good church.

I knew that the *only* way I could be successful in business was if I aligned my life and relationship with God. Despite having walked away from God for nearly thirty years, something inside of me—a hole—could not be filled by anything else. I had tried a myriad of ways to fill the void, including alcohol and spending money. But none of them seemed to work. Deep down, I sensed that this void could only be filled by having, and committing to, a relationship with God.

Within a few weeks, we were invited to church, and in January 2005, both Kay and I gave our hearts to the Lord. We accepted Jesus into our lives and made a commitment to have a relationship with Him.

I'd like to say that our lives changed instantaneously, but instead, our relationship with Jesus gained momentum over time. Within twenty-eight months of making that decision, we became debt-free! And I'm talking about a large six-figure debt that was removed like a millstone from around our necks. (How God worked miracle after miracle in our lives to get us debt-free is a story for another book!)

Would You Break Bread with a Vagrant?

My journey of faith really took off towards the end of January 2007, when my church kicked off the New Year with a Leadership Weekend. The theme that year was 'Paint the Town Red'. It was all related to going out into the community and performing random acts of Christian kindness.

Sitting in the congregation, enjoying the praise and worship, I started to thank God for the blessings I had received in my life. With my arms raised in praise, I was reflecting upon the wonders of God and the miracles He could deliver. With a sense of surrender, I heard God speak to me.

"Give *me* your burden and take on *mine*," the Lord told me.

"Sure, I'll give you my burden," I replied. "I want to become debt-free. I'll give You *that* burden, God. After all, that was Your idea! I've tried everything I can to go debt-free, but it hasn't worked out. Good luck. I hope You can do it! Now tell me, what burden do You want me to take on?"

"Be salt and light," was all that God said.

"Give me a break—what's *that* supposed to mean?" I enquired.

God defined His burden through the scripture in Matthew 25:31-46, which He summarised to me with the following phrase, "When I was hungry, you fed me; when I was naked, you clothed me; when I was in prison, you visited me...."

"Yep, I can do that," I replied. And with that, I took on my commission from God.

Within a week, I was walking down Queen Street at lunchtime. As I headed to McDonald's, I had to step off the curb to avoid a lady who was talking to a vagrant who was begging for money on the sidewalk. A little irritated at my detour, I walked up to the counter and surveyed the menu in anticipation of my order.

Then that all familiar, small, still voice started to talk to me. "What do you think you are doing?" it asked.

"Ordering my food," I replied, but I knew the question was not related to my proposed food intake. It was directed towards the vagrant who made me risk life and limb to avoid the oncoming traffic as I tried to sidestep him.

"But I'm in a suit," I said, pathetically trying to plead my case.

Needless to say, my conscience pricked me, and I walked straight out to see the vagrant sitting cross-legged with his back against the wall. Once I gained his attention, I politely asked him if he would like to join me for lunch since I wanted to buy him something to eat. The grin on his face was worth the price the meal cost. For an hour, I sat beside him, listening to him share his story. I didn't judge him; I just tried to bless him.

You might be thinking to yourself, "Well done, Elias. What a saint you are!"

Trust me; I'm not a saint! However, I'm sure you have heard of Mother Teresa. Now most of us will agree that she's a saint.

Mother Teresa began teaching history and geography in Calcutta at St. Mary's, a high school for the daughters of the wealthy. She remained there for fifteen years and enjoyed the work, but she was distressed by the poverty she saw all around her. In 1946, Teresa travelled to Darjeeling for a retreat. It was on that journey that she realised what her true calling was: "I heard the call to give up all and follow Christ into the slums to serve Him among the poorest of the poor."

The more you analyse Mother Teresa's story, the more you realise that she, like many others before and after her, started her journey to make a difference after she heard from God. Would you be willing to give it all up to follow the path put forward by God? What sacrifices would you be willing to make? And what reward could you expect to receive?

Mother Teresa's first year in the slums was particularly hard. She had no income and no way to obtain food and supplies other than begging—quite a comedown given that she was used to a life of comparative comfort. Often tempted to return to convent life, she had to rely on her determination and faith to get herself through it. The result—she helped thousands of people and became an inspiration to the world.

Would Free Advertising Help Your Business?

My journey of faith has not been as extreme as Mother Teresa's. But my blessings have exceeded my expectations year after year.

Not only did God make me debt-free in less than two years, but He enabled me to expand my investment portfolio during the recent Global Financial Crisis (GFC) by giving me 100 percent mortgages during a period when the banks were not lending a penny. You can read more about that in Key #21 "Taking Action Is Important". By borrowing other people's money, I was able to generate an income stream that is increasing my net worth on a daily basis.

In 2015, I was introduced to Gary Hoogvliet. He is the Head of Media at Rhema Broadcasting Group—New Zealand's major Christian broadcaster.

A towering figure—his website claims he is 8' 3" tall!—Gary met me for coffee one day as we discussed his potential journey within the speaking industry. As we spoke, I tried to position how his expertise could be used to add value to the audiences he would speak to.

Towards the end of the conversation, I navigated the discussion to a topic dear to me. I asked Gary for suggestions on how I could get a message that affected the youth in our country out to a wider audience. As I explained the concept, Gary stared intensely, hanging on my every word. By the time I finished speaking, Gary asked me whether I could summarise that message in sixty seconds.

With the challenge accepted, I came up with a total of seven messages, each around 140 words in length, which I submitted to him for review. To my surprise, they were accepted, without change, and I was asked to come in to the studio and record them.

With the addition of a soundtrack, they became 'Godspots'. In effect, these were sixty second spots that Rhema Broadcasting Group could play across its three radio stations. I had scored myself free advertising!

Remember, this score was achieved by a boy whose father called him an idiot and whose teachers said he would most likely end up in prison. Now what's *your* excuse?

What Is Your Secret Name?

A good friend of mine, author, life coach, and speaker, Kary Oberbrunner, wrote a book called *Your Secret Name*. According to BabyNameWizard.com, Kary is "originally a pet form of Caroline (full-grown), Carey is now commonly bestowed as an independent given name and is often confused with the Irish Kerry (black-haired one). The name is also used as a pet form of the various names beginning with the element Car-." That is somewhat unfortunate since Kary is a man—not a woman.

I was introduced to Kary by chance when we were both invited to join a teaching call by the president of the John Maxwell Team, Paul Martinelli. Kary lives in Columbus, Ohio in the U.S. and I live in Auckland, New Zealand—a distance of nearly 13,500 km. We were first introduced on the live call, and from the moment I heard Kary speak, I knew he had an amazing story to share.

As I researched Kary, I grew more fascinated by his journey. Bullied as a young boy for having a girl's name, Kary began to self-harm himself. He hid that throughout his childhood and into his adulthood, including his time in seminary college as he studied to become a pastor.

He eventually found comfort in God's Word and the teaching in the Bible. What God revealed to Kary eventually set him free from his self-injury.

In his book, *Your Secret Name*, Kary shares how we cannot know our true identity until we allow God to enter our lives. Let me summarise it:

Did you know that we have three names?

Our first name is our 'Birth Name'. Elias. Kay. Tom. Sarah. It's given to us when we are born.

Our second name is our 'Given Name'. Idiot. Fat. Anorexic. Bankrupt.

This name tends to define our identity—both positive and negative.

Our third name is our 'Secret Name'.

In Revelations 2, verse 17 God says, "I will give that person a white stone with a new name written on it, known only to the one who receives it."

What if there was a way to receive that 'Secret Name' this side of eternity? How would that affect your true identity? How would you live your life differently with that knowledge?

I believe that the enemy uses these 'Given Names' to lie to us. They steal our true identity and cause us to live a lie. I suffered under that lie for nearly 50 years. It robbed my self-esteem. It stole my confidence. It took away my career and stunted my growth. Sometimes you have to establish your relationship with God to discover your true identity.

If you feel that you may be living a false identity, take a few minutes to complete the following exercise. Think through the different nicknames you grew up with, or, if possible, draw on conversations that have had a negative effect on your life. It may feel uncomfortable, but I believe this exercise is worthwhile and can become cathartic on your leadership journey.

WHAT GIVEN NAMES HAVE BEEN SPOKEN OVER ME?	WHAT IMPACT HAVE THESE GIVEN NAMES HAD ON ME?

Applying lessons from Nelson Mandela's life:

Key #18 - GIVING IT OVER TO GOD

In 1952, the ANC designated a more activist era, which was ushered in with the election of a new president—Chief Albert Luthuli. Mandela had first met him in the late 1940s. A few months prior to his election, Luthuli was dismissed from his position as an elected and government-paid tribal chief.

Luthuli was a proud Zulu chief, a devout Christian, and an uncompromising leader in the struggle against apartheid. Once Luthuli was dismissed from his post, Mandela made the following observations about Luthuli, who issued a statement of principles called 'The Road to Freedom is via the Cross,': "[H]e affirmed his support for nonviolent passive resistance and justified his choice with words that still echo plaintively today: 'Who will deny that thirty years of my life have been spent knocking in vain, patiently, moderately and modestly at a closed and barred door?'"

Whilst Mandela did not profess to be a Christian, he held Christian values and was surrounded by strong Christians like Chief Luthuli. Even Jesus Christ was forced to expel the moneylenders from the temple. It is my belief that we should lean not on our own understanding, but that of a higher being to help us select the path less trodden....

"...they attempted to show that I was not a Christian either by asserting that the Reverend Martin Luther King never resorted to violence.... Even Christ, I said, when he was left with no alternative, used force to expel moneylenders from the temple."

— Nelson Mandela

Key #19

INCLUDING REGULAR CELEBRATIONS IN YOUR ROUTINE

"The celebration...you cannot practice it or anything.
It's a moment when the excitement of your
goal makes you react to the moment."

— Peter Bondra

We are in the home stretch. Only a few more keys and this part of the journey will come to an end. Before I tackle this key, let me remind you that we talked about recognising and rewarding good behaviour earlier. In this key, I want to encourage you to become more deliberate in how you implement celebration in your routine. Celebration goes beyond acknowledgement. It is a fundamental way of lifting your spirit and giving you some more motivation to keep taking action.

What Are Other People Seeing in You?

A few years ago, I was on the road delivering a keynote for a client. It was a busy schedule as we went from one city to the next. Halfway through the tour, we arrived in Christchurch where I was due to present just after lunch.

The room was oversubscribed, so there was standing room only. I stood up towards the back of the room and waited until the CEO had completed his opening address to the company. I could sense a level of growing excitement in this group. The fact that we had standing room only heightened the energy in the room.

Eventually, I was introduced, so I made my way to the front of the room and started to deliver my presentation. I was practically standing on top of my audience. A lot of eye contact was made, everyone was receptive, and the interaction was engaging. When I asked for a show of hands, the majority went up. As I nodded my head, everyone nodded in agreement.

Throughout the presentation, I noticed a person in the front row who was paying particular attention to me. He seemed to hang on every word I shared.

My presentation was about the power of accountability partnerships. I was sharing on the benefits that my clients and I had accomplished as a result of implementing the partnerships. In my presentations, I use a five-step process I have trademarked called the SHUN™ system (which I will outline later in this book). With a flourish, I closed my presentation with the comment, "What happens in your future, starts right now, when you take ac-SHUN™!" and I walked off stage to a chorus of applause. It was a wonderful feeling.

After my presentation, everyone took a short break for afternoon tea. Members of the audience streamed past me, many congratulating me for an entertaining and educative presentation. The person I had noticed from the front row stayed back until we were the only two people in the room before he approached me.

"I really enjoyed your presentation," he said. "And I could tell that you've benefited from these accountability partnerships yourself."

"How so?" I enquired.

"Because I was looking at your $600 shoes and your expensive watch," he replied. "You must be earning a lot of money to afford them!"

I thanked him for the compliment, and we continued to talk for a while. But I didn't have the heart to confess that my Fossil watch was purchased at an outlet mall in Pennsylvania and that my shoes cost me $70 to re-sole and re-heel, twice the price I originally paid for them!

People judge a book by its cover. That man measured me as rich and affluent because he placed an inflated metric on my outward appearance. He measured me at approximately ten times my real value. My strategy to look affluent had paid off since he went on to engage me as his personal coach. I was able to celebrate the small investments that led to more profitable business.

LIST THE THINGS YOU SHOULD CELEBRATE!

How Much Time Are You Taking to Celebrate Your Surroundings?

Over the last five years, I have been travelling extensively overseas. I have spoken in Australia, Singapore, Malaysia, the UK, and the U.S. In most cities, I have been based in the hotel where I have spoken, and in many cases, I would fly into the city the night before I was due to speak.

Where I had family living in the city, I would try to stay with them. This gave me a couple of extra days to spend with loved ones, and it helped me to reduce some of my expenses whilst I was travelling overseas.

As a frequent visitor to the East Coast of the U.S., I would try to combine a family visit with business. To ensure that I visited all my family members, I would have to spend at least a night with each sibling and his or her family, whilst keeping my uncle and his family happy by camping in their house. This was never a simple task since there was at least an hour's drive between each household. Yet, despite the distances involved, I never thought of it as a chore.

In 2015, I was in the U.S. en route to the UK when my father, whose health had been deteriorating, passed away. It wasn't a shock to us, and I was blessed that my wife, Kay, and my eldest daughter, Gabriella, were able to take time off work and travel from New Zealand to attend his funeral.

Kay extended her trip to escort me to the UK and back through Phoenix before we returned home.

"Since we're in New Jersey, we might as well take a trip to New York," Kay announced.

The thought had not crossed my mind before, but I took the opportunity to make a day of it. Kay had researched the day-trip, and I knew we were in good hands.

The following morning, we drove across town, parked our car behind Kings Super Market, and took the bus to Port Authority in New York. It was close to Times Square, so we navigated on foot and via the subway until we got to Ground Zero. It was an emotional place to visit given my experience on 9/11.

Our next stop—The High Line—was a 2-km-long New York City linear park built in Manhattan on an elevated section of a disused New York Central Railroad spur called the West Side Line. It is a truly stunning walk that captures the essence of New York City, both modern and old.

Since the High Line was a reasonable distance from Ground Zero and it was pouring with rain, I suggested we take the subway. "Definitely not!" said Kay. "How will we take in the sights and sounds of all that New York can offer from underground? You know, Elias, you travel a lot, but you aren't a traveller!"

The statement floored me. I stopped to analyse it and realised that she was right. I would come in to town, stay in a hotel, deliver my presentation, and then leave the following day. I might explore within a small radius of the hotel (even on the rare occasion I had a car), and often, it would involve going to a shopping mall to get some food to eat from its food court.

As a leader, do you spend time getting to know more about the culture of the places you visit? Or are you more interested in getting in and out efficiently? Do you nurture relationships with the locals, or do you choose to live like a hermit crab within the shell of your hotel room?

Take the time to celebrate the local culture and drink in the sights and sounds. Put aside some extra time and money to invest with the locals. Try to plan ahead and make sure you can connect with a host to take you around for a short excursion. It doesn't have to cost much, but it can develop lifelong friendships and memories.

Do You Get Recognised in Your Hometown?

I'm all for celebrating our heroes. If you travel across the U.S., you will often see that Americans recognise their military, which I applaud them for. They celebrate the sacrifices they have made to serve their nation.

Celebration is an important aspect of leadership. We need to find more opportunities to celebrate our successes, no matter how small they might be.

Often, when I am speaking internationally, I will have people come up to me and greet me like a long lost friend. Maybe I have a comforting smile or open body language, but invariably, they believe they already know me. Unfortunately, in most cases, it is the first time we have met.

On one occasion whilst in the U.S., I was getting ready to speak at a conference in Stamford, Connecticut when a gentleman came to sit at my table during the lunch break. No sooner had he sat down beside me than he turned to me and said, "I know you!"

I was intrigued since I didn't seem to recognise him.

"Where do you know me from?" I asked.

"You're on TV," he replied.

"Absolutely!" I chimed in. (Now, to the best of my knowledge, I have not been featured on TV in the U.S., but I wasn't going to spoil his perception!) With a high-five, we continued our lunch, and then I was asked to go with the MC to prepare for my introduction.

On another occasion, I was flying from Auckland to Christchurch. I sat in a window seat in the front row of the plane. Beside me was a young couple with their toddler. The father sat in the aisle seat, and his wife was in the middle seat with her toddler perched on her knee. He was a well-behaved child, and on the odd occasion, I would pick up the toy he had dropped and pass it back to his mother.

To occupy myself, I worked on a document I needed to edit, and within an hour, we had to prepare for landing.

As we were taxiing to our gate, the mother turned to me and said, "I'm sorry to be nosey, but I think I've met you before. Can you please tell me what you do?"

"I'm a professional speaker," I replied. "Maybe you attended a presentation I gave?"

She was convinced that she knew me, but once again, I had no recollection of having met her before. Who was I to rain on her parade? I went along with it and thanked her for her interest, stopping short of offering her my autograph!

Chance encounters like this have bolstered my self-confidence. Irrespective of whether these people knew me or not, I would celebrate the conversation and tell myself privately that I was a celebrity.

I've learnt it is important to celebrate the successes we have in life, no matter how small they might be. Each celebration helps to bolster your confidence, and as leaders, we must not only build up our own confidence, but that of our teams as well.

Are You Celebrating the Smallest of Wins?

Just after Kay and I started going to church, Kay was taking a walk on the beach when God revealed to her that she should give up her role as a consultant and look after the kids full-time. "But what about the money?" she said. "Don't worry; I'll take care of the money," God replied.

Kay came home and excitedly told me the news. "Really?" I squeaked before I cleared my throat and said, in a manlier, deep-throated guttural way, "Really!"

You have to realise she was earning a six-figure income. We had just bought a house with the corresponding mortgage, and we had chosen to give one tenth (a tithe) of our income to our church, following the biblical teaching of Jesus Christ. The concept of Kay giving up her income stream didn't sit too well with me!

A few days after she dropped this bombshell on me, I received a call from our client, who excitedly told me that his board had reviewed our proposal and wanted to engage Kay as its consultant. When could she start? I told him I thought Kay might be on another assignment, so I would confirm and get back to him.

I called Kay and told her the news. It was a six-week assignment, and it was worth nearly $40,000. What a test! Without hesitation, Kay told me she wasn't available, so she had to decline. After I had finished crying, I called my client back and told him that Kay was indeed otherwise engaged and we would source another consultant for them.

Shortly afterwards, Kay and I were baptised, and once again, God shared a vision with her that within two years, we would be debt-free. For the next eighteen months, nothing significant seemed to happen. Yet, throughout the journey, we made sure we celebrated even the smallest of wins we achieved. That gave us enough motivation to keep moving forward and taking the action required to become debt-free.

And within the two-year timeframe, we did indeed become debt-free! All glory and honour goes to God for His miracle in our lives.

So as I conclude this chapter, can I encourage you to include celebration in your portfolio and to see the difference it can make to your journey as a leader.

Applying lessons from Nelson Mandela's life:

Key #19 - INCLUDING REGULAR CELEBRATIONS IN YOUR ROUTINE

At the age of sixteen, Mandela was taken aside by the regent and told that he would not spend his life mining white man's gold, never knowing how to write his name. It would become his destiny to become a counsellor to Sabata, the king of the Thembu, which necessitated his education.

Prior to Mandela's departure, a celebration was held to mark that Mandela had passed his Standard V and been admitted to Clarkebury. A sheep was slaughtered in his honour, and there was plenty of singing and dancing.

"[I]t was the first celebration that I had ever had in my own honour," says Mandela in his book, "and I greatly enjoyed it. The regent gave me my first pair of boots, a sign of manhood, and that night I polished them anew, even though they were already shiny."

Celebration gives people the motivation to keep going and to take some more action, which will help them to accomplish the revelation they have. As a leader, make celebration a strong part of your culture, and use it to shod your team members with new boots to help them along their journey....

"It is better to lead from behind and to put others in front, especially when you celebrate victory when nice things occur. You take the front line when there is danger. Then people will appreciate your leadership."

— Nelson Mandela

Key #20

AVOIDING EXAMPLES OF BAD LEADERSHIP

"A good leader takes a little more than his share of the blame, a little less than his share of the credit."

— Arnold H. Glasow

Having explored the elements that make up good leadership, I would be remiss if I did not address poor or bad leadership traits. This key needs to be addressed in every organisation—irrespective of size. We are seeing more high profile examples of leadership that blur the lines between good and bad. This key is designed to stimulate your thinking and to challenge the norm.

Did You Know There's No Such Thing as a Get-Rich-Quick Scheme?

When I lived in the UK in the early 1990s, I had a conversation with a friend who told me I could get access to a brand new CD player. It would only cost £150, which at the time was probably a third of the cost of the item at full retail. I was led to believe it was water-damaged stock that a 'mate' had happened to gain access to. The packaging had slight damage, but otherwise, the devices were in good working order.

Limited stock was available, and it was on a cash-only basis. To be honest, the offer seemed too good to be true.

Well, I think you can guess the rest of the story. Money was exchanged, and then I waited at the pub for the mystery contact to arrive with the goods. One pint turned into two, and soon the bartender was calling time and ushering people out as the bar was locked up. Needless to say, I never saw the CD player or my money again.

If it sounds too good to be true, then it probably is!

The leadership lesson I learned here is to trust your instinct and go with your gut feeling.

How Well Can You Control Your Emotions?

I'm a hot-headed individual. It's not something I am proud of. Some would say I inherited my dad's temperament.

Back in 2003, Kay and I visited the U.S. to have my son christened in the Greek Orthodox Church. This happened to coincide with my parents' fiftieth wedding anniversary, so they joined us on holiday in the U.S. to celebrate it with our extended family. It was a milestone we were looking forward to. Unfortunately, our holiday didn't start off on the best foot....

Our itinerary took us from Auckland to Los Angeles and through to New York. The flights and layover alone were close to twenty-seven hours, and on top of that, we had a two-hour drive to my sister's house. We arrived late at night, and we slept in the lounge on a blow up mattress. There was an eighteen-hour time zone difference between New Zealand and the U.S., and we ended up with a restless baby who was wide awake.

Despite our efforts to get our son off to sleep, there seemed to be nothing we could do. My sister and brother-in-law tried to help us, as did my mother. But the more we all tried, the more stimulated he became. It soon became evident that our strategy was counter-productive.

With the clock about to strike 2am, my father stormed into the living room. He told me I should be able to control my son and have more compassion for the house's other occupants. In effect, he said, "You're a useless father, Elias. Get it sorted!"

And that's when the trouble started. I was enraged. A red mist covered my eyes, and I let my father have it with both barrels. I argued with him, my angry words spraying spittle across his face as we went toe-to-toe, face-to-face. Kay had to hold me back from physically striking him.

As a leader, we need to be in control of our emotions. It is very bad form to let others intimidate us. We all have a hot button that, if pushed, can lead us to a tipping point, but we need to understand that others can use that to their advantage.

What is your hot button? How do you react when somebody presses yours? What signals about your character do you pass to your followers through your actions? What will others say about your character? Will you be accused of being somebody who is hot-headed? Somebody with a short fuse? Worse still, how will others judge your character based on what they witness?

Are You Above Judgement?

In Auckland, we had a mayor who was seeking re-election. A few days after the announcement of his successful campaign, with a 50,000 majority vote, a major story broke accusing him of marital infidelity. The story had explicit details of an alleged affair with a woman young enough to be his daughter.

The mayor confirmed the affair in a brief statement and said he would not be commenting further. "I don't intend to comment on the highly personalised allegations made.... But I do confirm that I had a relationship with a woman that lasted around two years," he was quoted. "I told my wife previously, and she and I are working through the issues privately. We are looking to protect our children as best we can. These are matters of an entirely personal nature and I ask that the media respect my family's privacy."

Irrespective of political leanings, the question many of us were asking on Talkback Radio related to the man's integrity. As a leader, what is expected of you and your behaviour 'behind closed doors'? The mayor confirmed the woman was not a council employee, but she served on a council advisory board and stood in that year's election for a local board.

As leaders, we have to remember that after we are gone, our character stays behind. People will judge you by your actions. Infidelity can be seen by one segment of the population as a sin, whilst another might accept it 'as the way of the world'. Either way, you need to understand as a leader that your actions can have consequences, and you need to be willing to live with them. Media coverage today can be brutal, and family members can become casualties.

Did He Have Sexual Relations with that Woman?

Sexual infidelity within political circles dates back many centuries. Stories of adultery, such as that between King David and Bathsheba in ancient Jewish history, abound. Even the

Kennedy administration was rife with rumour, but sweeping the stories under the carpet was the policy of the day.

In 1998, the highest profile American political sex scandal emerged, regarding forty-nine-year-old President Bill Clinton and a twenty-two-year-old White House employee, Monica Lewinsky.

The course of action in the lead up to the story breaking was the following quote from President Clinton:

> But I want to say one thing to the American people. I want you to listen to me. I'm going to say this again: *I did not have sexual relations with that woman, Miss Lewinsky.* I never told anybody to lie, not a single time; never. These allegations are false. And I need to go back to work for the American people. Thank you.

After a twenty-one-day Senate trial, President Clinton was acquitted on all impeachment charges of perjury and obstruction of justice. He was held in civil contempt of court by Judge Susan Webber Wright. His license to practice law was suspended in Arkansas and later by the United States Supreme Court, and he was also fined $90,000 for giving false testimony.

How did the President's actions and comments impact the view of his leadership?

In a December 1999 article, Arthur H. Miller at the University of Iowa commented:

> Many outspoken Republicans have raised questions about how the American people could continue to have confidence in their political leaders, government institutions, or the rule of law when a president who lied to the public, lied under oath, and obstructed justice remains in office.

> Others ask how they can explain this immoral behavior and thwarting of the law to their children, especially in light of all the salacious details that were made public in Special Prosecutor Kenneth Starr's report on the Clinton-Lewinsky affair.

It is a question that we, as leaders, need to ask ourselves. Is lying acceptable in a leadership role, and do leaders have a moral obligation to a certain code of conduct? I would like to think it is our responsibility as leaders to create the culture that our team, organisation, or country operates under. However, it is up to you to draw your own conclusions on the performances of these leaders and the longer-term impact they have on our society.

What Lessons on Forgiveness Can We Learn from Nelson Mandela?

South Africa was in sore need of forgiveness after apartheid, and Nelson Mandela gave the perfect lesson on how it could be done.

Having spent twenty-seven years in prison for trying to end white-minority rule through violence, Mandela became an emblem of peace by reconciling with the individuals who had been the instruments of oppression during his captivity.

Four acts of forgiveness by South Africa's first black president pointed the way forward for a divided country to become united.

1. **Mandela invited one of his former jailers to a dinner marking the twentieth anniversary of his release from prison.** Christo Brand, a jailer responsible for guarding him at Robben Island and then at Pollsmoor Prison, developed a relationship with Mandela, who said it "reinforced my belief in the essential humanity of even those who had kept me behind bars."

2. **He invited his former prison guard to his inauguration ceremony as South Africa president.** Prison warder Paul Gregory's "soothing presence" and "courtesy" marked him out as different to most of his colleagues in Mandela's eyes.

3. **Mandela had lunch with the man who tried to have him killed.** Percy Yutar, the state prosecutor at the 1963 Rivonia treason trial, demanded the death penalty for him. Mandela said that Yutar "had only been doing his job," after Mandela invited Yutar to dinner in 1995.

4. **He wore the Springbok rugby jersey at the 1995 rugby World Cup final.** Few symbols summed up oppression for Mandela and his ANC colleagues more than the hated green Springbok jersey. Black South Africans had previously been made to stand amongst fans cheering the opposition. By wearing a green jersey at the World Cup final in 1995, and presenting the trophy to South African captain Francois Pienaar, Mandela sent out a strong message to his ANC colleagues that it was time to put aside enmity and become a united country.

LIST THE RELATIONSHIPS YOU NEED TO FORGIVE (AND ASK FOR FORGIVENESS)

Applying lessons from Nelson Mandela's life:

Key #20 - AVOIDING EXAMPLES OF BAD LEADERSHIP

In the wake of his father's death, Jongintaba, the regent, had offered to become Mandela's guardian. That act effectively benefited Mandela as he was treated like the regent's other children and afforded the same advantages they had. Mandela and his 'brother' Justice, were involved in a web of lies that started after their father, the regent, had arranged marriages for them. It started by selling two of the regent's oxen to a local trader without authority, then organising travel documents through a magistrate under false pretence, and lying to the chief induna (or headman), Piliso, who worked at the Crown Mines in Johannesburg.

Whilst the regent had previously sent a letter months earlier making arrangements for Justice to get a clerical job, Mandela was an unexpected package. Further lies secured them jobs as mine policemen, with the promise of clerical posts in the future. Unfortunately, Mandela was unable to contain his deception and bragged about their dishonesties.

"Flushed with our success," wrote Mandela, "Justice and I boasted of our cleverness to a friend of ours.... We explained how we had run away and tricked the regent into the bargain. Although we swore this fellow to secrecy, he went straight away to the induna and revealed our secret."

Their plan had backfired and Mandela and his brother were about to get their comeuppance. Mandela noted: "A day later, Piliso... reached inside his desk and pulled out a telegram. 'I have had a communication from the regent,' he said in a serious tone of voice, and handed it to us. It contained a single sentence: 'send boys home at once.'"

Lying gets you nowhere, and it did Mandela no good at that

point in time. As a leader, you need to be on the right side of the law, and it goes without saying that honesty is the best policy. Avoid being drawn into the web of lies that will lead you into a maze of deceit….

"We had no rejoinder for Piliso, and we sheepishly walked out of the office, feeling even more humbled than we had on the first occasion."

— Nelson Mandela

Key #21

TAKING ACTION IS IMPORTANT

"What happens in the future starts right now,
when you take Ac-SHUN™."

— Elias Kanaris

This is the last key I want to write about. To me, it is one of the most important leadership keys you will come across. You have invested time and money to read this book. Hopefully, it has done more than just tickle your fancy. I hope it has stimulated you to think more about how you lead others and how you can improve your leadership effectiveness. The trouble is that for most people, this is where our paths will part. Whilst everybody will have the same opportunity to put these keys into action, only a small percentage of readers actually will. The question is, "What are *you* willing to do?"

How Much Wealth Are You Sitting On?

An urban myth says that property values double every seven to ten years. Do you ever wonder whether that is true?

I live on the North Shore of Auckland, in a region known as the East Coast Bays. I was fortunate enough to move into my current home in 2005, when the property market was going through a slight lull. According to a report at the time this book went to press, Auckland boasted a total of fifty-nine suburbs that had an average valuation per house sale of over *one million dollars*! That represents nearly a third of the city.

One suburb, Herne Bay, already averages $2.13 million per house sale. St Marys Bay and Remuera look to soon crack the $2 million benchmark, having reached average house prices of $1.94 million and $1.79 million respectively.

It might seem mind-boggling for you to consider paying over $1 million for a property, and I certainly could not have comprehended that level of investment back in 2005. When I purchased my house, we paid in the region of half-a-million dollars for it, and even then, I had to take a big gulp when I signed the Sale & Purchase Agreement. Thankfully, I was able to become debt-free early in 2007, so the worry of paying off a large mortgage didn't weigh heavily on me.

Around the same time, I left the corporate world to become the Family Party's Party President, and since it was a voluntary position, Kay and I saw a dramatic reduction in our household income.

After the General Election, I started my own business in 2009. Coincidentally, that was during the Global Financial Crisis (GFC), considered by many economists as the worst financial crisis since the Great Depression in the 1930s.

When you add up the pieces, we had a smaller household income, I had no financial track record in my business, and we were in the middle of the worst financial crisis since the Great Depression. Banks were ultra-cautious on lending any money. So what did I do...? You guessed it; I decided it was time to invest in the property market.

Many financial advisors would probably direct you away from that strategy, but I approached my bank with the intention of exploring the possibility. To my surprise, they approved a 100 percent loan for the purchase of my first investment property!

Within six months, I had the chance to purchase a second property, and once again, I secured another 100 percent loan. With this came an introductory email from my new personal account manager. The bank now classified me as a high net-worth customer!

How did this happen? It goes against *all* logic that I should receive 100 percent funding to expand my portfolio in such a short time. The answer lies in the term 'leverage'.

I had already built up enough equity in my personal property that the bank knew it could offset the lending risk against holding the title on my house.

My property portfolio has continued to grow and between 2013 and 2015 I had my property valued twice. I was staggered to find out that it had appreciated more than 40 percent in less than twenty months!

From a leadership perspective, the value of your leadership is also increasing or decreasing over time. What are you doing to help your value as a leader appreciate?

How Can 20,000 Kilometres Increase Your Income by 700 Percent?

In 1995, I made the decision to move from the UK to New Zealand. It was a bold move since I had no job to walk into, a limited network of people in the country, and life savings of less than $15,000.

The preparation for my move was to scan the Kiwi newspapers—*The New Zealand Herald*, *The Dominion Post*, and *The*

Press—at the New Zealand High Commission in London. I researched job opportunities and open homes to gain insight into what I could expect.

With my eyes open and expectant, I came across an advert in the *Daily Telegraph* for a New Zealand-based recruitment agency that was interviewing in London. I quickly set up an interview with them. The meeting was positive enough, but no guarantees were made.

Inside a few months, I had arrived in Auckland and my first interview was set up. A week later, I was in Wellington, where a second interview was set up for me with Telecom New Zealand. The head of marketing met with me, and we spoke at length about an emerging business opportunity.

"We have an aggressive competitor in the market who is taking market share away from us," the marketing manager explained. "They are able to cherry pick our products and services. Discounting our 0800 services by a cent a minute, or reducing the access charges, etc. This is eroding our margins and putting some of our customers at risk. What we'd love to do is to create a new solution called 'Call Centres'. These will include the hardware, access, tolls, and 0800 services, making it more difficult for our competitor to cherry-pick individual services. How do you feel about heading up the team to review this and develop a strategy for us to use as an investment platform?"

With a rush of blood to my head, I replied without hesitation, "Absolutely! This is similar to the solutions we were developing in the UK. I can see how we can put this together and make it work...."

The interview concluded after an hour-and-a-half. All indications were positive, and a handsome remuneration package was mentioned. Happy and motivated, I shook hands with my interviewers and headed back down the maze of lifts and stairwells to exit at ground level.

No sooner had the doors to the building shut firmly behind me than I pulled out my cell-phone to call my ex-colleagues in the UK. The ring tone echoed for an eternity before the call was answered.

With a brief pause to exchange pleasantries, I rushed out my questions: "Do you know someone I can talk to within the team who knows anything about 'call centres'? I think I've just landed myself a job here, and I'll need to up-skill myself as quickly as possible...."

With my immediate mission accomplished, I pulled out a local map to get my bearings. I needed to head to the train station. As I rotated the map in my hands—hoping it now pointed in the same direction I was facing—a stranger walked past me.

"You look a little lost, mate," the Good Samaritan said. "Where are you headed?"

"I'm trying to get to the train station," I replied. "I think it's this way." And I pointed to my left.

"Good try, but no cigar!" the Good Samaritan chuckled. "You'll need to head in the other direction, where I just came from."

As the Good Samaritan started to give me directions, he abruptly stopped and said, "Tell you what; why don't I walk you there? It'll be easier than giving you the directions!"

I was pleasantly surprised by this generous offer of assistance. "Are you sure? It looks like you'll be going out of your way!"

The Good Samaritan beamed a hefty smile and reassured me it would be okay.

Strong leaders will recognise that they do not have to know the answers to all the questions. Nor do they need entire knowledge prior to embarking on a project. They need to be strong enough to ask for help and astute enough to know whom to engage with and what questions to ask.

But it has to start with action—a leap of faith, an ability to swallow your pride. What self-limiting beliefs are holding you back from asking for help? Take the time to list them below.

And what steps are you willing to take to change your beliefs? A journey of a thousand kilometres starts with a single step.

THE SELF-LIMITING BELIEFS I WANT TO CONQUER!

STEPS I WILL TAKE TO CONQUER MY SELF-LIMITING BELIEFS

Is Your Word Your Bond?

When you attend the certification program for the John Maxwell Team (JMT), it includes a session in which John Maxwell shares about the culture of the JMT—something he calls the JMT-DNA.

Maxwell is lending the program attendees his name as a lever to gain acceptance into the market. That carries a lot of responsibility as one of his certified speakers, coaches, and trainers. Now, with over 10,000 represented in the JMT worldwide, it becomes even more important for us to understand Maxwell's heart as well as his work ethic.

There is no doubt about Maxwell's credentials as a leadership authority. He has authored over 80 books and sold more than 25 million copies. He has spoken over 10,000 times, trained more than five million leaders, and is a recipient of the Mother Teresa Prize for Global Peace and Leadership from the Luminary Leadership Network. Maxwell speaks each year to Fortune 500 companies, presidents of nations, and many of the world's top business leaders.

What might not be known is that he has only cancelled his speaking obligations on less than a handful of occasions! That's because he is a man of integrity and known for his word. He even fulfilled an obligation to speak to an audience within a few days of breaking his leg and being in a cast. To facilitate this, he asked to be provided with a stool he could sit on to ensure he was more comfortable and didn't have to put weight on his broken leg.

This act, it turned out, helped him to identify a presentation technique that improved his ability to connect with his audience. He turned a limitation in his ability into a strength.

How Much Would You Have Paid for a Share in McDonald's Back in 1961?

In 1961, Ray Kroc, a milkshake machine salesman, bought the exclusive rights from Dick and Maurice McDonald to McDonald's for $2.7 million. Kroc subsequently turned McDonald's into an American institution and global entity.

Kroc's story illustrates the Law of the Lid. John Maxwell details that so well in his book *The 21 Irrefutable Laws of Leadership.*

Back in 1937, Dick and Maurice opened a small drive-in restaurant in Pasadena, California, located just east of Glendale. Their tiny drive-in was a great success, and in 1940 their business exploded. Annual sales reached $200,000, when they decided to move the operation to San Bernardino, a working-class boomtown fifty miles east of Los Angeles.

By the mid-1950s, annual revenue hit $350,000, and the brothers were splitting net profits of about $100,000 each year.

Whilst the McDonald brothers' genius was in customer service and kitchen organisation, when they tried marketing the McDonald's concept, their effort was a dismal failure. The reason was simple: They lacked the leadership necessary to make a larger enterprise effective.

The McDonalds' association with Kroc started in 1954. As soon as Kroc visited the store, he had a vision for its potential. In his mind, he could see the restaurant going nationwide in hundreds of markets. He soon struck a deal with Dick and Maurice, and in 1955, he formed McDonald's Systems, Inc. (later called the McDonald's Corporation).

As a leader, Kroc recognised that he needed to take action to capitalise on the potential he saw. In the early years, Kroc sacrificed a lot. He went without salary during his first eight years with McDonald's. He gave up his country club membership, put in long hours, and drew against his life insurance to fund the salaries of key people he wanted on his team.

Where can you apply extra effort that will pay dividends to you? Are you missing out on some opportunity because you don't think you have the credibility to lead that organisation? Like

Kroc, maybe you should take the time to do an inventory analysis of your leadership skills to determine how best to use them to leverage opportunities that appear to be out of your reach.

WHAT ARE MY KEY LEADERSHIP STRENGTHS?

Would a Cheque for $1 Billion Make You Cry with Joy?

In an interview with Reuters, Richard Branson, best known as the founder of Virgin Group, which comprises more than 400 companies, recalled crying when he sold the record label more than twenty years earlier for $1 billion.

"Of course, it was very hard—it's like selling your children," Branson said. "I mean, you build something from scratch, we had just signed Janet Jackson, we had just signed the Rolling Stones when we sold it, and I remember running down Ladbroke Grove, tears streaming down my face with the check for a billion dollars."

At the time of the sale, Branson had already diversified through the creation of Virgin Airlines. But a combination of the impact of the Gulf War, a recession, and a costly battle with British Airways forced Branson to sell Virgin Records to the then Thorn-EMI in 1992.

The decision to let go of his 'baby' was not one Branson took lightly. It was a business strategy that was executed to release the much-needed cash flow necessary to sustain his aviation enterprise.

Taking action can sometimes be a very painful experience—

emotionally as well as physically.

As a leader, you need to be strong enough to differentiate between the economic benefits and emotional pull of a decision. There will be times when you have to consider relinquishing control of one thing for the benefit of the wider organisation—similar to amputating a diseased body part to ensure someone's survival.

Strong leaders are able to make the decision to amputate one aspect of their business for the betterment of another.

Take time now to make an inventory of what you currently have on your plate that you should be releasing. Identify the key projects you want to accomplish and prioritise them to your top five. Ask yourself, "Will working on this task help me to accomplish my goals for my business?"

Once you have listed all of your activities, classify those you can relinquish. Look at this list and determine whether, like Branson, you could find a third party who would benefit from purchasing that from you. Maybe you can walk away with a cheque in your hands that could lead you to tears of joy....

KEY PROJECT	BENEFIT	KEEP IT	KILL IT	PRIORITY

Are You Taking Action or Waiting for Motivation?

Let me take you through a system I have discovered called the 5 SHUN™s.

The first "SHUN™" is 'Informa-SHUN™'. I can give you information, which by itself is nothing more than pure data. It is meaningless until you analyse it. That will lead you to your second SHUN™—'Revela-SHUN™'. That's when you get your aha moment!

The trouble with revelation is that, whilst you can easily get your aha moment, you shouldn't be like Bill Murray in the film *Groundhog Day* where you repeat the same aha day after day. There is nothing more frustrating than that!

It's okay getting an aha moment, but unless you get into 'Ac-SHUN™'—your third SHUN™—it's very hard to steer a parked car.

You say, "But Elias, don't I need to have motivation first?" No, 'Motiva-SHUN™' follows action. It is the fourth SHUN™, and it is important to note that it has to follow Ac-SHUN™. Most people fail with their goals because they wait for motivation to kick in *before* they get into action!

You don't have to know where the whole staircase leads to; you just have to find that first step. In fact, 'Celebra-SHUN™' is the fifth and final SHUN™. I think it is the most important of my 5 SHUN™s because, with celebration, no matter how small the win, you can celebrate your achievements, which can supply your motivation to continue in action.

As you read this book, I hope it represents more than just Informa-SHUN™. I hope that you have received your Revela-SHUN™ and that it encourages you to get into Ac-SHUN™. Please don't wait for Motiva-SHUN™—that's like waiting for the planets to align or for that perfect storm to appear. You could be waiting a long time. And remember to include a lot of Celebra-SHUN™ as you take this journey.

Let me conclude by telling you, "What happens in your future, starts right now, when you take Ac-SHUN™!"

Applying lessons from Nelson Mandela's life:

Key #21 - TAKING ACTION IS IMPORTANT

In 1970, Colonel Piet Badenhorst was appointed as the new commanding officer (CO) of the prison. He was reputed to be one of the most brutal and authoritarian officers in the prison system. With the removal of study and free time before his tenure even started, the expectations of his regime became apparent. He would roll back every privilege the prisoners had won over the years.

In 1971, a troika of judges—Jan Steyn, M.E. Theron, and Michael Corbett of the Cape provincial division of the Supreme Court—came to the island. Mandela was selected to be a spokesman for the prisoners. Prior to the meeting, he reliably heard that a prisoner in the general section had been severely beaten by a guard.

At the meeting, the judges indicated they would talk to Mandela privately, which he rejected, requesting that General Steyn and Badenhorst attend, adding that "it would be only proper for them to have the opportunity to reply to my charges."

As Mandela recounted the recent assault, Badenhorst shifted uncomfortably in his seat, asking in a gruff manner whether Mandela had witnessed the assault. Replying calmly that he had not, Mandela simply acknowledged that he had trusted his sources. Badenhorst once again threatened Mandela for talking about things he hadn't seen, telling him it would get him into trouble.

Ignoring Bandenhorst's comments, Mandela turned to the judges and said, "If he can threaten me here, in your presence, you can imagine what he does when you are not here."

Mandela's actions resulted in Badenhorst being transferred off the island within three months of the judges' visit. By taking the right action, you too can remove obstacles from your path to ensure your team's safe passage....

"Once, one of the warders, a very pleasant young man named Warrant Officer Brand, actually took me to his family's flat and introduced me to his wife and children. From then on I sent his children Christmas cards every year."

— Nelson Mandela

A FINAL NOTE

TAKING YOUR SHORT WALK TO FREEDOM

Now that you have finished reading this book, what are you going to do? What actions are you going to take? Which Leadership Key are you going to work on first? Which self-limiting beliefs are you going to change? How are you going to get the most out of the people you lead? How are you going to impact your team, organisation, or country?

As I said in the Introduction, this book is not the biography of Nelson Mandela. This book is about taking your leadership skills to the next level where you can influence other leaders around you, where you can empower them to help lead with influence. It is about helping you to apply Nelson Mandela's character traits and wisdom to lead more effectively.

The quality of your leadership has a direct effect on the value of your company's stock. Studies have shown that a company with good leaders can increase company stock by 900 percent over a ten-year period. The flip-side of the coin is that a company with a poor leader is reflected by a measly 74 percent increase across the same period. By now, I hope you can understand how your leadership style affects your stock's value and what the effect is on your key people.

Maybe you now realise that leadership has a profound impact on those who surround you. You can see why a staggering 37 percent of employees have cited bad leadership as the main reason why they have left a job. You can understand why 39 percent of employees feel underappreciated at work, whilst 77 percent of employees stated they would work harder if given more recognition!

By now, you may realise that whether you have people who report directly to you or not, you are a leader. Even if you are surrounded by people who can impact the profitability of your business and your take-home paycheque, you now know you can affect another outcome. You may have thought about the top two or three things that frustrate you the most about what happens in your business. And you can see that most of them relate to individuals in either the way they behave or their attitudes.

As a result of reading this book, maybe you can relate to the following:

You no longer have to be frustrated by the people who surround you. You know you can do a better job than your coworkers, but you no longer have to. You have discovered techniques you can use to stop you from becoming irritated when waiting for others to complete a task, or when they hand something back to you, you have learned you don't have to redo it. You believe you could take more time off and enjoy yourself with your loved ones without being concerned that if you took too much time away from your business, you'd come back to an even bigger mess. You believe you can make more money to invest in the things that will help you grow your business, or better still, in the luxuries you believe you deserve.

If you related to any of those changed self-beliefs, I feel your gain. Fortunately, you now know you're not alone.... Now you know that others have sat in the same seat as you not so long ago. Now you know you are not surrounded by individuals who were sent to torment you. You know it is up to you to lead them until they make contributions that outperform your imagination. What you now know is that I have faith in you. In fact, I believe you can break others out of the prison of their limitations.

As a result of reading this book, you have learned that:

- Everything rises and falls on leadership
- What you say has tremendous power on the outcome of your business
- Making a profit is good
- Developing relationships is easy
- You will improve your profitability by walking in your client's shoes
- You can set the pace of your success by leading from the front
- You will reduce your headaches by surrounding yourself with people you can trust
- You will increase customer satisfaction by doing the right thing
- Your successes will be directly related to recruiting people with a good attitude
- Learning never stops and is your responsibility
- Allowing people to make mistakes is good for your business
- Your key people will stay loyal as a result of nurturing relationships with them
- Your strength will come from overcoming obstacles
- Your biggest successes will come as a result of developing good daily habits

- You can get further, faster by planning ahead
- Encouraging your people is important
- You can get things done more easily by regularly rewarding good behaviour
- You can accomplish more by giving it over to God
- You can motivate and retain key people by including regular celebrations in your routine
- You can learn what not to do by avoiding examples of bad leadership
- Taking action is important
- Your life is now on public display and even the slightest slip can be costly

I now challenge you to apply the wisdom offered in this book. Then you can start liberating your leadership potential by jail-breaking your self-limiting beliefs so you can lead more effectively with influence. I want you to draw some lessons from Nelson Mandela's life that you can apply to your leadership journey.

If, like me, you have been stuck in a jail of self-limiting beliefs, or if you have team members who are locked in that jail, I hope this book has given you the keys to unlock the beliefs that have imprisoned you. By using those keys, you can achieve your aspirations. Maybe, like Mandela, you need to review your thinking and determine how it can affect your ambitions. Maybe, like Mandela, you need to say to yourself, "I want to be free. And so I let my insecurities and self-limiting beliefs go." Maybe, like me, you can let yours go and accomplish more for your life, your business, your team, or even your country.

I hope you have made this book your personal property and used the blank sections I've left for you to write your thoughts down. Your interactive participation, by completing the exercises placed in this book, will dramatically improve your leadership capacity and your retention of the material, which will impact your business and the key people who surround you.

I'm an executive coach, and I know the personal value that having a coach has had on my life. I'd like to coach you personally through your journey as you aspire to grow as a leader. I would be thrilled to offer you a no-obligation, complimentary 30-60 minute executive coaching consultation to help you liberate your leadership potential. We can have the consultation by phone, Skype, Zoom call, or in person if geographically possible. The best way to reach me is to send me a text on my private cellphone number at +64 21 615 449 or by email at Elias@EliasKanaris.com. Please give me your name and your time zone so we can schedule your complimentary executive coaching session. Due to spam, I would prefer that you text me instead of emailing me.

I wish you all the best as you start your personal journey to change your self-limiting beliefs so you may lead more effectively and with influence. Now is the best time to start liberating your leadership potential because your future begins when you take Ac-SHUN™!

FREE RESOURCES

Here are some free resources that you might want to access.

Lifting the Lid on Leadership: How You Can Keep Key People and Make More Profit

As I mentioned in this book, everything rises and falls on leadership. If you want to thrive in volatile times, it is important for you and your leadership team to take stock of your actions and determine the effect they can have on your bottom line. Get these wrong and they can lead to the following issues:

- Reducing your ability to retain key people within your team
- Destroying your brand in the marketplace
- Increasing customer churn

Leadership has a dramatic impact on the profitability of any company. Statistics show us that 37 percent of employees have cited bad leadership as the main reason why they left a job; 39 percent feel under-appreciated at work, whilst 77 percent of employees stated that they would work harder if given more recognition!

In my free e-book, *Lifting the Lid on Leadership: How You Can Keep Key People and Make More Profit*, you will pick up real strategies to help protect your key relationships and retain staff members who will strengthen your company and improve your profits. This e-book will serve as a useful tool to assist you in leading teams, whether in a corporate, government, or not-for-profit sector. It is designed to help you retain key staff and help you grow your profits. Whether you are starting your journey into leadership or are a seasoned professional, there are many gems included in these pages that you can implement immediately to help expand your business.

Download a complimentary copy of *Lifting the Lid on Leadership: How You Can Keep Key People and Make More Profit* at http://bit.ly/1P21FMH

Leadership to a Tea

I have interviewed a number of successful businesspeople and created a video blog called "Leadership to a Tea". The videos are short, 7–10 minute insights into these businesspeople's thinking and wisdom. You can access them here: http://bit.ly/25xMTqB.

You can also subscribe to a monthly email that will notify you when new videos are released at http://bit.ly/1sprrG3

Daily Motivational Quote:

Welcome to the Daily Motivational Quote! It's my pleasure to help you start your weekday with a motivational quote that will lift you to another level and provoke a positive thought about your upcoming day.

I hope you will enjoy reading them and using them for the positive impact they can give you and those who surround you.

You can access the Daily Motivational Quote at http://bit.ly/1VtBC7N

RECOMMENDED READING

Branson, Richard. *Losing My Virginity: How I Survived, Had Fun, and Made a Fortune Doing Business My Way.*

Burg, Bob. *Winning Without Intimidation: How to Master the Art of Positive Persuasion in Today's Real World in Order to Get What You Want, When You Want It.*

Carnegie, Dale. *How To Win Friends and Influence People.*

Chapman, Gary. *The 5 Love Languages: The Secret to Love That Lasts.*

Collins, Jim. *Good to Great: Why Some Companies Make the Leap...and Others Don't.*

Collins, Jim. *How the Mighty Fall: And Why Some Companies Never Give In.*

Covey, Stephen. *The 7 Habits of Highly Effective People: Powerful Lessons in Personal Change.*

Ferguson, Alex. *Alex Ferguson: My Autobiography.*

Franklin, Jentezen. *Believe That You Can: Moving with Tenacity Toward the Dream God Has Given You.*

Franklin, Jentezen. *Right People, Right Place, Right Plan: Discerning the Voice of God.*

Graham, Billy. *A Motivational Memoir: Your Ship Came in the Day the Doctor Smacked Your Bum.*

Hill, Napoleon. *Think and Grow Rich.*

Holtz, Lou. *Winning Every Day: The Game Plan for Success.*

Hyatt, Michael. *Platform: Get Noticed in a Busy World.*

Littauer, Florence. *Personality Plus: How to Understand Others by Understanding Yourself.*

Mandela, Nelson. *Long Walk to Freedom: The Autobiography of Nelson Mandela.*

Maxwell, John C. *Everyone Communicates, Few Connect: What the Most Effective People Do Differently.*

Maxwell, John C. *5 Levels of Leadership: Proven Steps to Maximize Your Potential.*

Maxwell, John C. *Good Leaders Ask Great Questions: Your Foundation for Successful Leadership.*

Maxwell, John C. *Intentional Living: Choosing a Life That Matters.*

Maxwell, John C. *17 Essential Qualities of a Team Player: Becoming the Kind of Person Every Team Wants.*

Maxwell, John C. *Leadership Gold: Lessons I've Learned from a Lifetime of Learning.*

Maxwell, John C. *Sometimes You Win; Sometimes You Learn: Life's Greatest Lessons Are Gained from Our Losses.*

Maxwell, John C. *The 15 Invaluable Laws of Growth: Live Them and Reach Your Potential.*

Maxwell, John C. *The 21 Irrefutable Laws of Leadership: Follow Them and People Will Follow You.*

Maxwell, John C. and Jim Dornan. *Becoming a Person of Influence: How to Positively Impact the Lives of Others.*

McCullough, Mamie. *I Can. You Can Too!*

Mooney, Allison. *Pushing the Right Buttons: People Skills for Business Success.*

Mortlock, Peter. *Grateful: 30 Years of City Impact Church.*

Oberbrunner, Kary. *Your Secret Name: Discovering Who God Created You to Be.*

Pease, Allan. *Body Language: How to Read Others' Thoughts by Their Gestures.*

Pease, Allan. *Questions Are the Answers: How to Get to 'Yes' in Network Marketing.*

Rath, Tom. *StrengthsFinder 2.0.*

Schwartz, David J. *The Magic of Thinking Big.*

Snow, Patrick. *Creating Your Own Destiny: How to Get Exactly What You Want Out of Life and Work.*

Tracy, Brian. *Eat That Frog: 21 Great Ways to Stop Procrastinating and Get More Done in Less Time.*

Welch, Jack with John A. Byrne. *Jack: Straight from the Gut.*

Wishart, Ian. *Eve's Bite: Seductive, Deceptive and Dangerous; the Trojan Horse Ideologies Poisoning Our Country and Destroying the West.*

ABOUT THE AUTHOR

ELIAS KANARIS is an author, professional keynote speaker, executive coach, leadership trainer, and entrepreneur. He has been a regular keynote presenter and M.C., and he has frequently spoken to audiences in the I.T., telecommunications, insurance, financial services, real estate, and education sectors in the UK, U.S., Italy, Singapore, Malaysia, Australia, and New Zealand. Since the early 1980s, Elias has been using humour and energy to deliver great learning experiences to his audiences. His articles have been published in *Market$hare Magazine*, *New Inceptions*, and *Leadership Inspirational Magazine*.

Elias has a Master in Science in Medical Electronics from the University of Wales, Institute of Science and Technology (UWIST), and he has a Bachelor's Degree in Electrical and Electronic Engineering from Kingston University.

He has been the senior consultant in the I.T. and Telecommunications sector, where he was part of a team responsible for his company's top twenty-four clients, which billed $450 million per annum. Elias is also a founding partner of the John Maxwell Team (JMT)—the largest and fastest growing leadership training organisation in the world. He has served as a member of the President's Advisory Council (PAC) and was a founding member of the Peer Review Team on the JMT. Elias is currently serving as the national president for the National Speakers Association of New Zealand (NSANZ). He is also a member of the Executive Committee of the Global Speakers Federation (GSF), where he has also represented NSANZ.

Elias was born in North Africa, was educated in the UK, and now lives in Murrays Bay in Auckland, New Zealand. He lives within five minutes walking distance from a beach and enjoys the lifestyle most people dreamt about in their youth.

CHECKING ELIAS KANARIS' COACHING AVAILABILITY

Research from the International Coach Federation indicates that professional coaching brings many wonderful benefits, including marked increases in productivity and a range of interpersonal skills that lead to increased customer satisfaction and a strong return on investment.

People who are coached comment that they get fresh perspectives on personal challenges, enhanced decision-making skills, greater interpersonal effectiveness, and increased confidence. And the list does not end there. Those who undertake coaching can also expect appreciable improvement in productivity, satisfaction with life and work, and the attainment of relevant goals.

Professional coaching maximizes potential and, therefore, unlocks latent sources of productivity. Research shows that coaching:

- Improves work performance by 70 percent
- Increases business management by 61 percent
- Improves time management by 57 percent
- Improves team effectiveness by 51 percent

Building employees' self-confidence so they can face challenges is critical in meeting organisational demands. By investing in an executive coach, it has been shown that:

- Self-confidence can be increased by 80 percent
- Relationships can be improved by 73 percent
- Communications skills can be improved by 72 percent
- Life/Work balance can be improved by 67 percent

Executive coaching generates learning and clarity for forward action with a commitment to measurable outcomes. The vast majority of companies (86 percent) say they at least earned back their investments.

I have been supplying executive coaching services since 2011, and I have provided thousands of hours of coaching to clients across the manufacturing, insurance, financial services, direct marketing, telecommunications, and real-estate industries. I have helped my clients to qualify for MDRT (Million Dollar Round Table), achieve their business and personal goals, and become better organised.

Virtually, all companies and individuals who hire a coach are satisfied. Altogether, 99 percent have been "Somewhat" or "Very Satisfied" with their overall experience, and 96 percent claimed they would repeat the process.

If you are serious about making a change in your life, I would love to be your executive coach. The good news is that it won't cost you anything! Buying milk or bread from the supermarket costs you because after you drink the milk or eat the bread, it's gone! But with executive coaching, you receive a return on your investment. I've seen my clients increase their revenues by 120 percent or even as much as 380 percent!

I'd like to offer you my platinum executive coaching for life option. It includes a one-hour personal executive coaching call each month for the rest of your life. You also receive one hour of group coaching calls per month for the rest of your life. In addition, you receive five three-minute leadership teaching videos via email per week for the rest of your life. And the investment for this platinum executive coaching for life program is available for a one-time investment of $48,000. If you want to make that payment up front, the total investment will reduce to only $39,000.

Before you say, "YES!!!" to my platinum executive coaching for life program, I would be thrilled to offer you a no-obligation, complimentary 30-60 minute executive coaching consultation by phone, Skype, or Zoom call, or in person if geographically possible. The best way to reach me is to send me a text on my private cellphone number at +64 21 615 449, giving me your name and time zone so we can schedule your complimentary executive coaching session.

For more information about my executive coaching services, visit one of my websites listed below and then text me your name, time zone, and the best time to redeem a 30-60 minute, no-obligation, executive coaching consultation by phone, Skype, or Zoom call.

www.EliasKanaris.com

www.LiberatingYourLeadershipPotential.com

www.CoachEliasKanaris.com

Mobile: +64 (0)21 615 449

BOOK ELIAS KANARIS TO SPEAK AT YOUR NEXT EVENT

When it comes to choosing a professional speaker for your next event, you will find no one more respected or successful—no one who will leave your audience or colleagues with a more renewed passion for life—than Elias Kanaris, one of the most gifted speakers of our generation. Since 1986, Elias Kanaris has delivered more than 2,000 inspirational presentations worldwide.

Whether your audience is 10 or 10,000 in New Zealand or abroad, Elias Kanaris can deliver a customised message of inspiration for your meeting or conference. Elias understands that your audience does not want to be "taught" anything, but is rather interested in hearing stories of inspiration, achievement, and real-life people liberating their leadership potential.

As a result, Elias Kanaris' speaking philosophy is to humour, entertain, and inspire your audience with passion and stories proven to help people achieve extraordinary results. If you are looking for a memorable speaker who will leave your audience wanting more, book Elias Kanaris today!

To see a highlight video of Elias Kanaris and find out whether he is available for your next meeting, visit his website at the address below. Then contact him by phone or email to schedule a pre-keynote phone interview:

www.EliasKanaris.com

www.SpeakerEliasKanaris.com

Elias@EliasKanaris.com

Mobile: +64 (0)21 615 449